VIRGINIA SATIR

THE PATTERNS OF HER MAGIC

VIRGINIA SATIR

THE PATTERNS OF HER MAGIC

STEVE ANDREAS

SCIENCE AND BEHAVIOR BOOKS, INC.
PALO ALTO, CALIFORNIA

Library of Congress Card Number: 90-063678

ISBN: 0-8314-0076-5

Editing by Steve Beitler
Cover Design by Lynn Marsh
Interior Design by Gary La Rochelle/Flea Ranch Graphics
Typesetting by TLC Graphics
Production Editing by Jim Nageotte
Printed in the United States of America.

I would like all of us to live as fully as we can. The only time I really feel awful is when people have not lived a life that expressed them- selves. They lived with all their "shoulds" and "oughts" and their blaming and placating and all the rest of it, and I think, "How sad."

—VIRGINIA SATIR (1989)

I once was with somebody I liked very much—an older person, when I was considerably younger than I am now. That person said, "Spend at least fifteen minutes a day weaving dreams. And if you weave a hundred, at least two of them will have a life." So continue with a dream and don't worry whether it can happen or not; weave it first. Many people have killed their dreams by figuring out whether they could do them or not before they dream them. So, if you're a first-rate dreamer, dream it out—several of them—and then see what realities can come to make them happen, instead of saying, "Oh, my God. With this reality, what can I dream?"

—VIRGINIA SATIR (1984)

To
Richard Bandler

Without your brilliant and persistent demonstrations and teaching over the past dozen years, I would have noticed very little of what is written here.

Contents

Foreword

During the past fifteen years, it has been a rare pleasure and an honor to have built models of some of the best communicators of the last generation, including people such as Moshe Feldenkrais and Milton H. Erickson. But most of all, it has been a pleasure to have started out by modeling Virginia Satir, the originator of conjoint family therapy, master therapist, master teacher, and most of all, master communicator.

I remember many, many years ago, sitting in my driveway in Soquel, California, working on a car. Looking up from the frustration of difficulty with the engine, I saw a very unusual person. She walked down my driveway and up to me, unlike most of the people I have met in my life, who were unsure of themselves, uncertain, or nervous, especially when they were in unfamiliar surroundings. Virginia Satir possessed none of these qualities. She was equally at home on a stage, with a family, with a schizophrenic, or in just about any context in which she had the ability to communicate, something she did so exquisitely.

Virginia also demonstrated the difference between caring about the work one does and caring about the prestige that one gets from such work. During the past fifteen years, I have met many other therapists who were famous—famous for intellectual work, or famous for things that they may or may not have done in years past. In contrast, Virginia was a worker. I never knew her to have a bad day, to be "off," to do anything but give a hundred percent—all the time. Some people criticized her for her lifestyle, but I'm not one of them. I envied her energy and her willingness to commit fully to everything she did. As long as I knew her, she persevered and demonstrated an abundance of both heart and skill.

What Steve Andreas has set out to do in this book is something like what I attempted to do over fifteen years ago. When I set about writing *The Structure of Magic*, I had just spent a month with Virginia in a place called Cold Mountain Institute. I was struck by how powerful a communicator she was, and how successful she was in her own work. I was also impressed with how little other people were able to learn to do what she did. They would imitate her tonality or her jargon, but rarely did they take the time to learn and to imitate her skill. This isn't because people are bad, or because—as Virginia put it—"we are all slow learners," but because they did not realize how precise she was in her communication. Although Virginia communicated—as she said, "highly intuitively"—that did not change the fact that she was precise about every word she chose, every gesture and movement she made. Virginia understood that communication came from the full range of experience, and that it was linked to people's pasts, from before they were born. And that it set a course and a direction for the future of not just individuals, but for entire families.

There was a time when Virginia had to hide the fact that she did family therapy. She said she was just "interviewing" families before she did therapy. Fortunately for all of us, those days are gone. Virginia created an opportunity for us all to explore and grow and change in new and exciting ways. Those freedoms are available to all of us as professional communicators, for some of us as psychotherapists, and for some of us just as people who want to learn to be able to do more in life at every opportunity. Virginia serves as a powerful model of someone who lived her life to the fullest. Yet at the same time that she did things for herself, she also did things for an abundance of others. Hundreds of thousands—perhaps millions—of people's lives will be changed because this woman gave her all to every piece of work she did.

In the transcript that Steve Andreas has analyzed here, he has taken to heart not only Virginia's caring attitude toward people, but the specific ways in which she achieves the outcome she seeks. The most powerful thing you can learn from this transcript is that Virginia never wavers from what she sets out to do. And what she sets out to do is what the client asks her to do. She tries everything she can, and everything she does relates directly to the client's desired state.

The terminology and the way in which Steve studies Virginia are perhaps different from how most people would, and perhaps similar to the way in which I would approach a study of her. But I think what this book offers the sincere student of Virginia Satir is more than just an attitude. It offers a profound example of how tenacious, persistent, and resourceful Virginia was, and at the same time, how precise and methodical. If Virginia was one of the people you ever envied in your life, or would ever want to emulate, rather than emulating her tonality, style, and jargon, or the kinds of things she said, I think it is time we got serious enough to emulate her skill. And that requires that we sit down and break it into pieces, and find out what this genius was doing, so that we can do the same kind of work with the same kind of tenacity and heart.

Steve, I think you have done a beautiful job. For those of you about to read this book, read on and learn. The wisdom of Virginia Satir will be worthy of study for centuries to come. I think this book stands as a real tribute to what she did and what she cared about. And although this is different from her own teaching style, as Virginia said, "We are all slow learners, but we are all educable."

—*Richard Bandler*

Introduction

Virginia Satir is almost universally acknowledged as one of the most powerful and effective therapists of this century. Throughout a career spanning some forty-five years, she developed systematic ways of helping people grow and change. Her remarkable warmth and precision in working with people was developed by her fine ability to observe what worked—and what didn't—to move people closer to their desired outcomes.

When learning from experts, it is usually much more important to observe what they actually do than it is to listen to what they say about what they do. Our descriptions of our own behavior are often biased and myopic, and we all know how to do much more than we can explain to someone else. This was particularly true of Virginia,* who was continually moving away from her psychiatric-based training of the 1940s, and intuitively pioneering new ways of helping people learn how to deal with life's inevitable problems.

Most therapists' descriptions of their therapy tend to be global and unspecific. Virginia, for instance, would talk about "gaining

*I have wrestled with the question of using Virginia Satir's first name or last name in this book. Using the last is often considered more respectful, but it is also more formal and distancing. Some might consider using her first name to be demeaning or patronizing. However, it is also more direct and personal, something Virginia was always working toward. I never heard anyone call her "Dr. Satir" in workshops; it was always "Virginia." Finally, I asked a number of people who knew her far better than I, and they all voted for "Virginia."

trust," "making contact," "building positive self-worth," and the importance of the "human connection" and an "I-thou relationship." Although she demonstrated these skills exquisitely, she was much less able to specify exactly how she accomplished them, either verbally or nonverbally. To learn how she actually achieved these things, we have to study her work itself.

Although few therapists are willing to demonstrate publicly what they do—they prefer to practice privately—Virginia was a happy exception. Not only did she conduct thousands of public demonstrations during her long career, she also freely allowed videotape recording. Probably as many videotaped hours of Virginia's work exist as of all other prominent therapists combined. Used with a verbatim transcript, a videotape makes it possible to analyze the fine details of verbal communication, the accompanying nonverbal communication—which is even richer and more complex, the ongoing interplay between the verbal and nonverbal communication, and the flow and sequence of the session as a whole. Repeated review brings an ever-deepening understanding of the process of change.

The heart of this book is a verbatim transcript of a seventy-three-minute videotaped session of Virginia working with a woman, Linda, in a weekend workshop held in 1986 at the peak of Virginia's power and skill, only two years before her death in September 1988. In this particularly moving individual session, Linda moves from great anger at and resentment of her mother to feeling compassion and love for her. A followup interview with Linda over three years later verifies the lasting positive impact that this session had on Linda's life and her relationship with her mother.

This session is particularly interesting for at least two reasons. Virginia was known primarily as a family therapist, and in family sessions she alternately focused her attention on different family members. In contrast, this session focused only on Linda, so it is much easier to follow the patterns and sequence of her work.

The second reason is that Linda was not an easy client. Although very expressive and willing to share her feelings, she also had what Virginia described during the session as "a highly developed ability to stand firm on things." Since Virginia had to work very hard to change certain understandings in Linda, we are treated to a particularly rich display of her versatility and persistence.

Commentary and descriptions have been added to the verbatim transcript to clarify and characterize what Virginia was doing at each point as she patiently leads Linda step by step toward forgiveness. The first chapter describes the important themes of Virginia's work, making it easier to understand their significance as they appear throughout the session.

Many therapists have the warmth and compassion that Virginia demonstrated so abundantly, yet they are largely ineffective because they don't know what to do. Others have technical communication skills; but without the nonverbal human qualities Virginia emphasized so much, their work is much less effective than it could be. Virginia is a particularly worthy teacher because she possessed warmth, compassion, finely honed perceptions, and specific skills and techniques.

To make sure his students had a little humility in using what he taught (something many might say he lacked himself), my old teacher Fritz Perls used to say, "Just because you've got a chisel doesn't make you Michelangelo." On the other hand, how much could Michelangelo have accomplished without any chisels at all? Imagine Michelangelo trying to carve a marble block with only his fingernails to release the vision imprisoned within the stone. Great work needs both the tools of the trade and the vision and humanity to direct those tools. Virginia Satir demonstrated an extraordinary measure of both. If we want to honor her genius, I know of no better way than to study her work carefully and learn how to do what she did so beautifully.

And I suppose that before I leave this world, one thing that I would wish for all the world to know, is that human contact is made by the connection of skin, eyes, and voice tone. These are the things that taught us before we had words. How our parents touched us, how they looked at us, what their voices sounded like, were all recorded in us.

—VIRGINIA SATIR (1989)

The Major Patterns
of Satir's Work

Certain attitudes pervaded everything Virginia Satir did. Knowing some of these essential elements of her work provides a useful orientation for understanding the verbatim transcript that appears in the next chapter. However, some readers may prefer to go through the transcript first without preconceptions and then return to consider the views presented here.

This chapter briefly describes sixteen major patterns of Virginia's work. Specific examples are provided, to avoid the ambiguities that pervade most descriptions of therapy. All examples or quotations are taken either from the transcript of a family session published in *Satir Step by Step* (Satir and Baldwin, 1983) or from the Satir videotape set "Family Relationships" (1989). The sequence in which the major elements appear is arbitrary and does not indicate relative importance.

This chapter is an expanded and revised version of the article "The True Genius of Virginia Satir," which appeared in *Family Therapy Networker* (Jan./Feb. 1989).

A Solution-oriented Focus on the Present and Future (in Contrast to a Problem-oriented Focus on the Past)

Although Virginia would listen to blaming and complaints about the past in order to maintain rapport with the speaker, she immediately turned the person's attention to solutions or outcomes in the present and future.

> I just want to find out right now for you, from you, what at this moment—never mind the past—what right at this moment would make life better for you if it could happen, living in this family? (1983, p. 68)

> That's what you *don't* like. Could you say what you do? (1983, p. 98)

> When people tell me what they don't want, I say, "Well, that's interesting; what do you want?" And it's very hard for people to form what they want. (1989)

> I want you to look at me now, and I want you to listen really carefully. There's a lot of history—I know there's a lot of history and I don't know what it is, and I have a hunch that oftentimes you don't see what's right in front of your nose, because it is all covered up with what you expect, because you almost did it right now. Are you with me? (*Margie:* Uh huh.) OK, now I'd like you to look at Casey and feel his skin through your hands at this moment and tell me what you feel. (Casey explodes into a smile.) (1983, pp. 112–114)

> I once was with somebody I liked very much—an older person, when I was considerably younger than I am now. That person said, "Spend at least fifteen minutes a day weaving dreams. And if you weave a hundred, at least two of them will have a life." So continue with a dream and don't worry whether it can happen or not; weave it first. Many people have killed their dreams by figuring out whether they could do them or not before they dream them. So, if you're a first-rate dreamer, dream it out—several of them—and then see what

realities can come to make them happen, instead of saying, "Oh, my God. With this reality, what can I dream?" (1984)

Virginia's work was guided by the basic outcome questions:
"What do you want?"
"How will you know when you've got it?"
"What stops you now?"
"What do you need in order to get it?"
She also understood that the answers to these questions have to be specified in sensory-based terms, not in vague generalizations or abstractions.

VIRGINIA: I'd like you, if you would, Casey, to say to Margie something you'd like from her—for her to change, some way, whatever it is.

CASEY: Stop attacking me. I mean you come on—it's an adversary relationship, babe, when you want attention, which turns me off.

VIRGINIA: I know you're talking from a whole lot of experiences. It's not very specific, but could you be specific? In a specific way, what would you like Margie to change dealing with you?

CASEY: Sure. Like when you and the kids want to go to the park, or when you want to go to the park with the kids. (1983, p. 120)

Virginia also knew that when someone wants others to change—no matter how reasonable the request might be—that automatically puts the person in a position of being helpless, dependent on others' willingness to oblige. To be useful and empowering, an outcome needs to direct the person toward what is in his own power to do. Questions such as, "What can you do that would get that response from him/her?" can refocus the person's attention on what *he* can do to make things better.

As one of the first people brave enough to see the whole family at once, Virginia also knew that each individual's outcome had to be specified in ways that made it desirable, or at least acceptable, to other family members. Once the client gave Virginia a positive outcome, she went after it tenaciously. When one intervention didn't work, she would try variations on that one, or different ones, until she got the desired results.

When Virginia did focus on the past, she usually utilized it to provide a vivid demonstration of patterns of interaction that continued into the present. At other times she focused on the past so that she could redescribe past events to give them a more positive and empowering meaning in the present.

Positive Intentions

One of the most powerful aspects of Virginia's work was her assumption that everyone's *intentions* were positive, no matter how horrible the behavior was, and her use of these positive intentions as a firm foundation of agreement from which to search for more positive feelings, communication, and behavior. On at least one occasion she facilitated a group that included both a Nazi death-camp survivor and an ex-guard from the same camp, successfully helping them to understand each other, and find their common humanity. Even when she did not verbalize it, Virginia always presupposed positive intentions and distinguished between intentions and behavior. She believed that, at the core, people mean well—even when they do mean things.

> I heard you say that this (yelling at the kids) started out with you trying to please Margie. (1983, p. 72)

> One of the things I'm discovering is a tremendous feeling of concern and caring from your father to all of you children, and from your mother to all of you children. But I don't think that always comes through as much as it could. (1983, p. 116)

Perceiving that someone has good intentions changes our response when the person is exhibiting problem behavior. It means we can agree with the person's intention and validate his humanity, even though we still don't like the behavior. Instead of bickering or fighting, we can join in a search for alternative behaviors that satisfy and validate *both* of us.

No Blame

Virginia never blamed anyone. She presupposed that hurtful or destructive behavior was simply a result of limited opportunities to learn how to respond more positively.

> . . . We learn from whatever our experiences are. OK? It's not because it is bad, it's just that we learn certain things. (1983, p. 82)

> You were mad. Well, those things happen sometimes. (1983, p. 26)

> OK. Now what if it would happen that none of this could happen without everybody's help? (1983, p. 62)

Virginia perceived the therapist's role as that of an educator: teaching and demonstrating how people could learn to perceive, respond, and act in ways that were more effective and satisfying.

> Problems will always be with us. The problem is not the problem; the problem is in the way people cope. This is what destroys people, not the "problem." Then when we learn to cope differently, we deal with the problems differently, and they become different. (1989)

As one way of communicating to people that their own experiences, whatever they were, were valid, Virginia often asked them to visualize a medallion made of something wonderful to them, to hang around their necks:

> On one side is written "No." And under "No" it says, "Thank you for noticing me, but what you ask doesn't fit for me right now, so the answer is no."

> And you turn it over, and on the other side it says "Yes." And then it says, "Thank you for noticing me. What you asked me fits wonderfully well, and the answer is yes."

And then when you get timid at a certain point in time, you take out your medallion, and you put the one [side] out that really fits. And then you look underneath, and you know what to say. (1989)

Teaching people simply to notice whether a request or invitation fits is self-validating. Responding with a simple yes or no avoids all the shoulds and oughts, incongruity, confusion, defensiveness, and blaming that so often occur when people try to appear to be different from what they are.

Equality

Virginia often used role-plays to demonstrate the destructive results of typical and traditional family patterns of dominance and submission. She also used role-plays to teach family members an alternative: communicating as equals. As a therapist, Virginia deliberately operated from a position of equality, both verbally and nonverbally. She would bend down so that she could speak to children eye to eye, and she often stood children and shorter people on chairs so that they could be on the same level as taller grownups. She continually demonstrated how much more satisfying it is to relate to others as equals.

Virginia often included herself as an equal in the family's struggles by using the pronoun "we." "I think we all have to struggle with that [controlling anger]." (1983, p. 38) "You know that whenever we get mad, it's hard to see anyhow." (1983, p. 22) Often she would mention an experience of her own that was similar to something that someone in the family was experiencing. By including herself in these ways, she provided powerful experiences of what some have called normalization: seeing difficulties simply as normal problems to be solved. When we have difficulties we often blow them out of proportion, and this makes them much more difficult to solve. Perceiving them as normal is often a major step toward resolution.

Another aspect of Virginia's teaching equality was her flexibility with roles: "Any one of us can be a teacher or a student to the other." (1989) This carried through all her work, and was particularly evident in the way she asked the family to correct her understanding of their interactions. Virginia was very direct, yet tentative, often restating what she had heard and asking the family to correct her.

> Let me see now if I hear you. That if your father—if I'm hearing this—some way that he brings out his thoughts . . . . He gets over-angry, you feel, or something like that? (1983, p. 34)

> OK. Let me show you a picture that I see at the moment. I just want to get the picture out, and then you help me to check it . . . . And this is my picture in my head from what I learned, and it may not fit at all, but it could. (She then goes on to create a "family sculpture" that illustrates her understanding.) (1983, p. 54)

> Let me play back, just so I know if I understand. Part of this piece of support for you would be if your children did more of what you asked them to do. Is that a piece of it? (1983, p. 70)

> This is what I heard you say before. Did I hear you correctly? (1983, p. 72)

When family members disagreed with each other, Virginia would say something like, "Everybody's got their own picture" (1983, p. 50) or "It is all right; these are human problems" (1983, p. 20). She thus validated everyone's experience and avoided taking sides in the family's right/wrong battle.

Virginia's favorite phrases for filling time as she paused to think were "OK" and "All right," which literally means "Everyone/everything is right."

When someone disagreed with her description of an experience, she would usually say simply, "Oh, so I was wrong," and ask the person to clarify. Or she would acknowledge the statement and move right on to something else.

Working from a position of equality as a therapist accomplishes three important things simultaneously. First, it shows how to sidestep the one-up/one-down, dominance/submission struggles that often disturb and complicate family communication. Second, it ensures that the therapist doesn't get caught in the family hierarchy and become part of the problem instead of part of the solution.

Finally, Virginia's emphasis on equality also has a much deeper significance. Fighting and disputes are always based on incomplete information and noticing differences. When conflicts are extreme, each side perceives the other as so different as to be inhuman. In contrast, understanding and compassion are built on fuller information and seeing the similarities between people. Virginia focused on commonalities among people to create an appreciation of how we are all similar in many ways. Virginia believed that with a broad enough base of common experience and understanding, any dispute could be resolved. In the next example, she first draws out the father's childhood experiences and then draws a parallel with his own son:

VIRGINIA: What did your father do, in your opinion, when you couldn't meet your idea of what he wanted?

CASEY: He insisted that I be responsible for my younger sister, and he insisted that I act like a man although he treated me like a child.

VIRGINIA: So that was kind of two messages. Be a man, but don't be a man.

CASEY: Yeah. What really turned him on was when I started racing motorcycles at twelve, and he thought that was machismo. He'd run around town introducing me to all his buddies, especially when I'd win a race. If I fell off or something, I was the bad guy. I had to take care of my sister.

VIRGINIA: That would be like Coby having to take care of Lisa and Lucy. That kind of thing? (1983, p. 80)

Providing Positive Alternative Choices

Despite centuries of the technique's failure, many people still try to stop problem behavior directly with some kind of punishment. If billions of rat hours have proven anything in experimental psychology, it is that punishment doesn't extinguish learned behavior. *Punishment only suppresses behavior by creating conflict between opposing motivations.* Most people have enough conflicts already; they don't need more. In contrast, Virginia knew that if you teach people satisfying ways to interact, they will simply not want to go back to painful and destructive ones. As Mammy Yokum said many years ago, "Good is better than evil, because it is nicer." Most therapists attempt to *subtract* problem behaviors. Virginia, instead asked herself, "What can I *add* to this person's life so he won't want to do the problem behaviors anymore?"

> I spend no time stopping behavior. I say, "That's a skill you've got. Now let's see if we can have some other ones." (1984)

> Instead of these being bad things, they only tell us what we had an opportunity to learn, that's all. And anything that's learned, we can leave it there, and we can learn something else. We don't have to unlearn one thing in order to learn another. It doesn't have to work that way. So we don't even have to bother about getting rid of the things we learned. What we have to do is learn what we learned, and then out of those things choose the things we want to learn better, or new things. (1984)

After Virginia helps the husband, Casey, elicit a positive response from his wife, Margie, by reaching out to her, Virginia says:

> Is that a new idea? That you could be that impactful to somebody? (*Casey:* Yeah.) So maybe there's a piece here for you to learn about what your impact really is. You've heard an awful lot about when you yell. You know that impact. But there's lots of other things. Here's one of them, so to know that piece, too. (1983, p. 120)

Reframing Behaviors and Perceptions

Virginia was justly famous for her ability to change people's perceptions of events so that they saw things more positively. This made problems easier to resolve. A mother's nagging became evidence of how much she cared; a father's punishment for curfew violations became loving protectiveness.

Once she worked with a woman who had been abused by her father when she was young. He had beaten her severely with a bullwhip, then took her to her grandparents' house, dumped her, and never came back. Virginia's reframe was that abandoning her in this way was the father's ultimate gesture of love. He realized that he was out of control, so he left her at the grandparents' house and never saw her again to avoid any possibility of hurting her further.

Virginia's presumption of good intentions, elimination of blame, and focus on desired outcomes are also powerful and pervasive reframes. They change the meaning of behavior and perceptions in ways that result in more positive feelings and more constructive behavior. There are two basic types of reframing: context reframing and meaning reframing.

Context reframing places a "problem" behavior in a different context, so that it can be seen as having value there. For instance, a father may think of his daughter's "stubbornness" as bad—until he thinks of it in the context of a man with bad intentions trying to take advantage of her. Every behavior can be valuable in some context. Even killing someone may be necessary and useful in self-defense. Context reframing depends on the therapist's ability to think of contexts in which the client is likely to see a "problem" behavior as valuable.

A next step is to validate the behavior in those useful contexts and then search for alternative behaviors in the contexts in which the same behavior causes problems.

Often Virginia described a problem behavior as a perfectly understandable response to a *past* context in which a person had limited information and understanding.

VIRGINIA: OK, now what you told me was that you had a beautiful experience in being parented by your father, and a pretty hellish one in being parented by your mother.

MARGIE: Right.

VIRGINIA: Now I want to tell you, Margie, what that says to me
. . . and maybe we can fill in the pieces. That you did not have a
model for how a woman could mother.

MARGIE: Right.

VIRGINIA: Okay, and that would say to me something else, that
there are some pieces left out in your self feeling good as a woman.

MARGIE: True, true. (1983, p. 78)

After establishing that someone's responses belong to an earlier context, Virginia would go on to change and add to the person's
perceptions and understandings, so that the person could have more
positive and useful responses in the present context.

Meaning reframing changes the meaning of a behavior while
keeping it in the same context. When a father yells at his son, the
son may think that the father sees him as bad or unlovable. Perceiving
that the father's intention is to make the son's life better, but that he is
limited in his ability to communicate because his own father was abusive, transforms the meaning of the yelling into something more positive. This will change the son's response to it, which in turn will
change the father's response. It is easy to yell at someone who is
sneering and looking away; it is much harder to yell at someone who
is smiling with appreciation.

Often Virginia would reframe simply by using different words to
redescribe a problem behavior. The connotations of the new description would result in more positive perceptions. Virginia redescribed
the father's angry behavior as "some way that he brings out his
thoughts." (1983, p. 34) When Casey's wife reaches out to touch him,
and he describes his feeling as "strange," Virginia redescribes it as "a
new thing." (1983, p. 110) Later in the session she redescribes criticism as an opportunity for learning: "So, when I ask you if you're criticizable, all I mean is, are you teachable?" (1983, p. 150)

I've heard that Virginia once said to a teenager who had gotten
two of his classmates pregnant, "Well, at least we know you've got
good seed." Saying this didn't condone his behavior; rather it made it
easier for her to bypass the blame, outrage, and attacks, and begin to
ally herself with the teenager so they could begin to work together
toward solutions.

12

Most of Bandler and Grinder's book, *Reframing* (1982), is a distillation of the reframing and negotiation patterns that Virginia used to bring family members into a shared and workable world. *Reframing* also describes procedures that make it easy to learn these essential therapeutic skills.

Action

Another powerful element of Virginia's effectiveness was her insistence on action. She understood that people change only if they fully experience the events or perceptions that words can only point to.

> Words don't have any energy unless they spark or trigger an image. The word, in and of itself, has nothing, nothing. One of the things I keep in touch with is, "What are the words that trigger images for people?" Then people follow the feeling of the image. (1989)

Virginia frequently pointed out that people tend to stay in, or return to, behavior that is familiar. Actively trying out a new behavior is one way to make it familiar; Virginia often suggested to people what to say and how to say it. She would sometimes even say it for them, demonstrating nonverbally exactly what she wanted them to do.

> As you move into new behavior and allow yourself to do it, it becomes familiar, so that a step toward change is to act "as if." Now it used to be a long time ago that to act "as if" meant that you were a fraud. Actually, what it's doing is giving our systems a new set of things to respond to. . . . Whenever I want to help people to do what's comfortable for them, instead of what they've been used to doing, then I help them plan some ways so that they can enact in front of me that new possibility. (1989)

After ten-year-old Lisa responds to her mother's crying by saying, "Everything was so sad and everything," (1983, p. 84) and that people in the family were feeling unwanted, the dialogue goes:

VIRGINIA: I'd like to make a suggestion to you, because maybe this could be helpful. I am going to find out if everybody in the family does know what it feels like to be unwanted, but I wonder what would happen if you felt that way and you said, "You know, right now I'm feeling nobody loves me." What do you think would happen if you put words to that?

LISA: Then my mom would probably say to me that she does love me.

VIRGINIA: Then maybe your mother would come to you and say she does love you? Would that help some things?

LISA (nodding):   It would just make me happy again.

VIRGINIA: It would make you happy again. OK. You're sitting down here, but I wonder if you could, just for practice, just so everybody could hear and you could hear: "Right now I am feeling nobody loves me." Would you say those words?

LISA: Right now I feel like nobody loves me. (1983, p. 88)

As family members tried out new ways of communicating, Virginia paid close attention to the nonverbal behavior to see if there was congruence. If she noticed incongruence, she would ask about their perceptions and feelings in order to make their experience and communication more complete and understandable. She especially asked about the feelings and yearnings that lay unspoken beneath the harsh words or the cold silence. Virginia assumed that such yearnings could be fulfilled through clearer communication.

> Now let me be sure. You have a look on your face which doesn't—I am not sure what you are feeling right now, Susie—whether you really feel this is a serious bargain? (1983, p. 48)

VIRGINIA: How did you feel, by the way, Margie, when Lisa came to you when you were crying?

MARGIE: Good.

VIRGINIA: Could you tell her?

MARGIE (looking at Lisa):   I felt good. I felt secure. (1983, p. 100)

After helping one or more family members make changes, she would ask them to re-engage in a live interaction, so that she could evaluate and test what she had done. Whenever Virginia noticed verbal or nonverbal behavior that could interfere with clear communication, she would stop to clarify it, showing people how to gather information and resolve objections. In this way, she taught how to "fine-tune" communication so that it elicited appropriate positive responses in other family members.

After checking with family members to confirm that they all feel unloved at times, Virginia asks the whole family:

What would happen if, when you were feeling it, you were to put words to it like Lisa just did? What do you suppose would happen with you, Casey, if you put words to that? "Right now I'm feeling nobody loves me."

CASEY: I have. I've put words to it before.

VIRGINIA: Those words?

CASEY: Well, "Nobody gives a shit about me."

VIRGINIA: Oh, that's a whole different thing. (Getting up and pointing a finger at Casey) Because you know what that means— "You should give a shit about me," and that doesn't say, "I'm feeling, at this point, unloved." (Sitting down, she still maintains eye contact with Casey.) (1983, pp. 90–92)

Virginia used action to translate hopes and yearnings into behaviors that satisfied them, making sure that the communication was clear and unambiguous, both verbally and nonverbally. As other family members responded, she would clarify their communication as well. After Margie expresses a wish to be closer to her husband, Virginia says:

So, if you acted on your wish—do it and see what happens. (Margie leans over and touches Casey's knee.) Now what you're doing—you could make that a lot easier if you moved over here.

MARGIE: OK. Instead of reaching out. (Margie is now sitting across from Casey, close to him, touching his knee, smiling at him.)

VIRGINIA: Now, I noticed something. Notice what happened when you did this. What happened?

MARGIE: He kind of shifted back a little.

VIRGINIA: Is that what you saw?

MARGIE: Maybe he didn't quite know how to feel.

VIRGINIA: I saw a couple of movements and I don't know. Then you can ask Casey what he thinks he did. I saw him first move forward and then a little back. (Looking at Casey) Is that what you were doing?

CASEY: Uh huh.

VIRGINIA: OK. How did you feel about Margie taking the risk of moving under her own wishes toward you?

CASEY: Strange.

VIRGINIA: OK. That's a new thing.

CASEY: Uh huh.

VIRGINIA: Now that you've gotten over the feeling of strangeness, how does it feel to have her here?

CASEY: Like it used to.

VIRGINIA: And that means. . . ?

CASEY: Well, it's nice.

VIRGINIA: I'd like you to tell her that.

CASEY: It was nice. Like a warm, fuzzy. . . . (1983, pp. 110–112)

Family sculpture was one of Virginia's well-known ways of transforming words into action. It helped her depict the family's system of interaction so that family members could see themselves more clearly. She would position family members in a still tableau or sculpture that displayed their typical ways of interacting—their supporting, clinging, blaming, placating, including, excluding, their distance and closeness, power and contact relationships, etc. (1983, pp. 54–62 and 96–98). Sometimes she added props, such as ropes, to dramatize the ways in which members restricted each other with rigid rules and roles, fears, "shoulds," and "oughts."

At other times the initial sculpture became a moving sculpture or "stress ballet," demonstrating a sequence of interactions between family members (1983, pp. 136–150). These simplified dramatizations provided family members with insight into the repetitive processes that characterized their interaction, regardless of content. When Virginia taught them new ways to interact, these changes would typically occur in a wide range of settings.

Virginia also moved around a lot herself in order to make physical contact with different family members in turn. She often interrupted unproductive interactions by getting between the participants and blocking their views of each other. (When I first saw Virginia in the early 1960s, three-inch heels and several inches of bouffant hairdo augmented her six-foot frame—truly a giant among therapists.)

By forcing family members to respond to her, instead of each other, it was easier for her to elicit more positive responses. After getting a better response, she would get out of the way and allow family members to interact again. When the couple in *Satir Step by Step* reaches an impasse in which they are each reacting badly to how the other looks, and Virginia wants to interrupt and work with the wife alone, she gets between the husband and wife, facing the wife:

VIRGINIA: OK. Now wait a minute. (Casey shakes his head, laughing with a disbelieving expression.) I am going to do this, right now (Virginia moves her chair in front of Margie, blocking Casey from Margie's view. At the same time Virginia moves her right hand in back of her in such a way that she touches Casey's knee.) because I want us to connect. You have a wish and your wish is. . . . I'm doing this on purpose, you know that (referring whimsically to the fact that she is hiding Casey). Uh, your wish is that you'd like to be in touching contact with him. (1983, p. 106)

After working with the wife to clarify what she wants, and dealing with her objections, Virginia moves aside and allows them to communicate with each other again, while she monitors their interaction.

Association/Dissociation

When a person recalls a problem situation, he can experience it in one of two very different ways.

In an *associated* memory, the person re-experiences the event fully, as if it were happening again now. He sees what happened again through his own eyes, and hears and feels what he felt at the time.

In contrast, a person can also recall a memory from a *dissociated* viewpoint, as if he were an impartial observer watching a movie or videotape of someone else experiencing the event. From a dissociated viewpoint the person sees and hears everything that happened, but his feelings are the much milder feelings that a detached observer might have.

Experiencing an associated memory of a problem evokes strong unpleasant feelings that provide powerful motivation for change. However, people often become stuck in these strong feelings and the single, associated viewpoint; this makes it difficult for them to change. People in this position are also usually oblivious to their own behavior and how this elicits responses in others that contribute to the problem.

A dissociated point of view frees people from the unpleasant feelings associated with a problem. This makes it easier to observe a problem more objectively and to respond more reasonably and creatively. From this viewpoint you can also review the same events while seeing your own behavior and how other people are responding to it. This literally provides a broader perspective with much more information about what a person can do to improve the communication or interaction.

To summarize: *association* evokes strong feelings that provide motivation for change, while *dissociation* provides less intense feelings, more information, and better access to creative resources that can help resolve problems.

Virginia was adept at using association and dissociation to build motivation and achieve change. When she wants the family to experience fully the pattern that she perceives—that everyone blames the father—she says:

> "Bad guy" feels like people are always pointing the finger. Let me give you my picture of what it might feel like to Casey, OK? Would you all stand up and point your fin-

gers at your father? No. Stand up and do it. All of you stand up and point at your father. (Everyone stands, pointing a finger at Casey.) If he would feel that in his insides, he could feel that, "Everybody thinks I am a bad guy." Is that what you feel?

CASEY: Yes.

When Virginia wants Casey to experience this even more fully, she asks the family members to continue for a while and asks Coby, the son, to "put it a little stronger."

VIRGINIA: Now look at these fingers for a minute. Point all those fingers at your dad. Put it a little stronger, Coby. Look at these fingers. And could you tell any one of these people how you feel about having those fingers pointed, Casey?

CASEY: Yeah, I don't like it. (1983, pp. 96–98)

By contrast, Virginia's reframing nearly always implicitly created a dissociated viewpoint, a new perspective on problems. By asking people to act out a family sculpture or ballet, family members associated into familiar roles. However, because Virginia relabeled behaviors and asked them to do them deliberately, they occurred in a new and broader context.

Each family member also sees himself participating in the ballet of family interactions. Although people tend to dissociate spontaneously, Virginia gave people explicit verbal instruction to be sure they made *pictures*. After setting up a sculpture depicting the pecking order of the kids in the family, Virginia says, "Just make a picture of it—that's right. OK, keep that [hand] down. We're just going to make like we're showing pictures." (1983, p. 56)

Talking about the sculptures as "pictures" makes them something to look at from the outside, giving family members a new dissociated viewpoint. When she finishes this process she turns to the mother and says, "Is this any sight you've seen, Margie?"

MARGIE: Very definitely. Yes.

VIRGINIA: Is this a sight you've seen, Casey? (Casey nods.)
(1983, p. 58)

Whenever a family member said anything positive, Virginia
would insist that he say it in a way that connected him directly with
someone else in a feeling way, to associate both people into the positive feelings of the experience.

VIRGINIA: OK, now I'd like you to look at Casey and feel his
skin through your hands at this moment and tell me what you feel.
(Casey explodes into a smile.)

MARGIE: Warm.

VIRGINIA: OK. Tell it to him, because he's there. I know all this
already.

MARGIE (looking into Casey's eyes):   You're warm and you're
soft. It feels good.

VIRGINIA: Now how do you feel, telling that to Casey? Right
now.

MARGIE: Good and whole.

VIRGINIA: And how do you feel, hearing it?

CASEY: It feels pretty good. (1983, p. 114)

VIRGINIA: Now when this happened, when Casey reached out
to you, like this, how did it feel?

MARGIE: A tingly sensation.

VIRGINIA: Tingly. Tell it to him. "You tingle me."

MARGIE (looking at Casey):   You tingle me. There's a tingling
sensation there. (1983, p. 118)

"A tingly sensation" seems to hang in space, unconnected to
anyone. "You tingle me"—despite sounding awkward—puts Margie
back into an associated, positive interaction with her husband. Notice
that Margie spontaneously goes back to dissociation with, "There's a
tingling sensation there."

Expressiveness

Virginia didn't just wait for people to respond positively; she actively elicited responses from family members by asking questions about feelings and perceptions that were not being expressed clearly, and by asking family members to shift positions and enact roles. Her nonverbal behavior was even more important in eliciting responses. Her legendary congruence and touching, her shifting voice tone, tempo and volume, and her facial and hand gestures were powerful nonverbal elements that created responsiveness in family members. As videotapes of Virginia demonstrate, few people could be in her presence and not be moved strongly in some way.

Whenever Virginia elicited positive responses, she immediately used them to reconnect family members with each other. This shared connection became a basis for resolving their difficulties. The excerpts in the previous section contain two examples of this, and others appear in the sections on "Action" and "Amplifying Positive Feelings and Behaviors."

Humor

One of the responses that Virginia elicited and used most frequently was humor. Her sessions were punctuated by laughter, even when the family was wrestling with issues that had caused them a great deal of unhappiness.

Humor is valuable for two closely related reasons: it is enjoyable and it lightens a person's feeling state. In a lighter state, people are more flexible and creative, with more personal resources available to resolve problems of living and relating. Even a very serious problem is easier to solve if you don't take it *too* seriously. (This is not to be confused with defensive humor that dismisses and ignores problems.)

When people have problems, they typically feel stuck in the problem, fully associated into it, with one unpleasant point of view, strong feelings, and no alternatives. When they can see the same situation in a humorous way—even briefly—it involves *seeing yourself—dissociated—in the situation rather than being in the situation.*

Humor literally provides at least one alternative way to view a problem. Even if this viewpoint is not useful, it is a much better place from which to start trying out *other* possible viewpoints (than being stuck in the situation). Humor can make it easier to experience other points of view and learn from them. The viewpoints of others involved in the problem are also useful, since those people probably have different perceptions and responses.

Virginia was a master at taking sensitive and painful subjects and treating them with humor. By contrast, most therapists—including many of her students—get too serious, too fast—and get stuck. Virginia took people through serious issues, but usually *after* treating these issues with humor. This allowed her to go back to the humor, lightening the seriousness and helping people experiment with new perspectives. By doing this repeatedly, Virginia taught people first how to acknowledge and express their feelings fully, and then to move to a lighter state in which it is easier to find solutions to problems.

"I find that the things that have the most fun are the most profound." (1984)

Shifting Referential Index

Association and dissociation can be used together to make it easier for a person to step inside someone else's experience and "walk a mile in his moccasins" in order to understand that person's perspective.

The first step is to dissociate from our own perspective and then associate into another person's point of view. Seeing events from someone else's perspective provides powerful information for resolving difficulties. This information can be especially useful when it is combined with a third, more objective perspective that shows you and the other person together interacting and responding to each other. Below is an exercise titled "Accessing Your Own Parenting Wisdom" that teaches people how to do this with children. This is excerpted from the "Parenting Positively" chapter in *Heart of the Mind* (1989).

First find a comfortable, quiet place where you won't be disturbed for a few minutes. Take a moment to relax and get comfortable, so that it's even easier for you to benefit from this process.

Step 1. Think of a difficult situation with your child. Perhaps your child has been doing something that you haven't known how to handle, or that drives you up the wall. Are you worried or concerned about some aspect of your child? Perhaps you will select something your child does, or it might be something about your child's feelings. You will get the most value from doing this if you pick something that happens repeatedly.

Step 2. Run your movie of this situation from your own point of view. Re-experience the episode. Imagine you are going through this situation with your child again. Start at the beginning, looking out through your own eyes, re-experiencing what actually happened. Notice what information is available to you, how you feel, and what you see and hear. If you are someone who doesn't "visualize," that's fine. You can just "sense" that you are re-experiencing this from your own point of view, and this method will work just as well. You may want to go through several examples of this situation.

Step 3. Re-experience this *same* situation again, but *as your child*. Run your movies of this situation from your *child's* position. Go back to the beginning of the same situation you re-experienced in Step 2. Stop your "movie" right before the situation started. Before you play the movie, *this time* look over at your child. Notice your child's posture, the way your child is moving, breathing, etc. Listen to the sound of your child's voice. Now *step into your child*. Take a moment to *become* your child. You are now moving like your child, seeing out of your child's eyes, and having your child's feelings. Let yourself take on this experience as you now let the movie of this situation go forward. If you're not sure you're "really" being your child, that's OK. Just let yourself do it, and notice what you can learn.

Take as much time as you need to go through this situation *as your child*, and notice what new information is available to you. Do you become aware of feelings your child may be having that you weren't aware of from your adult point of view? As your child, do you notice something your child wants or needs that you hadn't been aware of? What else do you learn by being your child? What sense do you get about what your child is experiencing in his or her own world, and how he or she is dealing with it?

What do you notice about your own behavior as you watch and listen from your child's position? Does your behavior seem different to you from this vantage point? For now, just take note of what you learn from doing this. If you notice that part of your own behavior seems very inappropriate from your child's position, you can be pleased that you got new and useful information. If you learn something about what your child may be feeling, you can be similarly pleased.

Step 4. Re-experience this situation as an "observer." Run the same movies again, but this time from an outside position. Watch and listen to that experience from a point of view that is off to the side, allowing you to see *both* yourself and your child at the same time. Observe the experience as if you were watching a movie of someone elsc.

Notice what you learn from this position. Do you notice something about the way you and your child respond to each other? How do things look and sound to you as an outside observer? What do you see more clearly about yourself and about your child? (1989, pp. 85–87)

In the transcript in *Satir Step by Step*, just after the son has said he'd like his father to be able to control his temper, Virginia asks the son, "Do you know what it feels like to be angry?" (1983, p. 36), and a little later, "I was wondering if you know anything about what it feels like to get angry." (1983, p. 38) Both these interventions invite the son to step into his father's feelings in order to gain understanding of how the two of them are similar. Although this was typically a major intervention of Virginia's, there are only a few examples of it in the older (1974) transcript in *Satir Step by Step*. However, there are many examples in the more recent (1986) transcript in this book.

Amplifying Positive Feelings and Behaviors, and Interrupting Destructive Communication

Virginia seized every opportunity to get family members to notice and express feelings and behaviors that would bring the family closer—carefully and patiently knitting the unraveled family back together with loving hands. Several of the excerpts provided in the sections "Action" (p. 12) and "Association/Dissociation" (p. 17) are excellent examples of this.

Virginia also took every opportunity to interrupt any communication that would tend to tear the family apart, usually with the direct command "Wait a minute" often drawn out or repeated. Then she would transform the disruptive communication into a positive connection. "Action" (p. 12) contains one example; here is another. Right after Casey says, "It was nice. Like a warm, fuzzy. . ." Virginia turns to Margie and asks, "How do you feel about that?"

MARGIE: I disagree with him.

VIRGINIA: What do you disagree about?

MARGIE: Whenever I approach him—"

VIRGINIA (interrupting):   Wait a minute, we're right here, right now. (MARGIE: Yeah, I agree.) I want you to look at me now, and I want you to listen very carefully. There's a lot of history—I know there's a lot of history and I don't know what it is, and I have a hunch that oftentimes you don't see what's right in front of your nose, because it is all covered up with what you expect, because you almost did it right now. Are you with me? (MARGIE: Uh huh.)

OK, now I'd like you to look at Casey and feel his skin through your hands at this moment and tell me what you feel. (Casey explodes into a smile.)

MARGIE: Warm.

VIRGINIA: OK. Tell it to him, because he's there. I know all this already.

MARGIE (looking into Casey's eyes):   You're warm and you're soft. It feels good.

VIRGINIA: Now how do you feel, telling that to Casey? Right now.

MARGIE: Good and whole.

VIRGINIA: And how do you (Casey) feel, hearing it?

CASEY: It feels pretty good. (1983, pp. 112–114)

Whenever anyone in the family expressed feelings that brought the family closer, Virginia would resonate with them. Her voice became softer, lower, quavery, and the d's tended to drop out of her speech. Later, when she wanted people to be in touch with their feelings, her voice would become soft and quavery again—a nonverbal invitation to become sensitive to feelings and express them.

Identifying Limiting Beliefs and Challenging Them

People in difficulties frequently see things in "black and white," and often express this in statements that are overgeneralizations. One clue to such limiting beliefs is the use of universal quantifiers—words like "all," "always," "whenever," "every," "totally," and their negations—"none," "never," etc.

One way to challenge an overgeneralization is to scale it down to a specific example. At one point in the *Step by Step* session, the dialogue goes:

VIRGINIA (to the wife): You just share with Casey at this point what you were feeling when he started to talk about this specific incident just now.

MARGIE: Hurt.

VIRGINIA: Hurt. OK. All right. Now, could you say what that hurt is about?

MARGIE: The family.

VIRGINIA: No, I mean right here. This is in here.

MARGIE: I hurt. Emotionally, I hurt.

VIRGINIA: And what made you hurt?

MARGIE (accusingly):   Because we don't have a father.

VIRGINIA: Now wait a minute. (Drawing out the words) Wait a minute. You're back into, if you'll forgive me, into a museum for the moment. I want to come back to something else. Just now I asked Casey to ask you for something, OK? And he went into something very abstract and I asked him to be specific. Now, was it the fact that Casey found something to criticize in you that made you feel hurt?

MARGIE: Yes. (1983, pp. 122–124)

In this segment, Virginia scaled back the overgeneralizations "hurt" about "the family," and "we don't have a father" to the mother's feeling bad about being criticized. In the process, Virginia also transforms Margie's general complaints about her husband into a statement about her own difficulty in dealing with criticism.

Virginia frequently asked other family members to give their views of an overgeneralization, inviting them to provide specific exceptions or counter-examples. And sometimes she would interrupt and bring the person back to the here and now without directly challenging the overgeneralization:

VIRGINIA: How do you feel about that?

MARGIE: I disagree with him.

VIRGINIA: What do you disagree about?

MARGIE: Whenever I approach him—

VIRGINIA: Wait a minute, we're right here, right now.

MARGIE: Yeah, I agree.

VIRGINIA: I want you to look at me now, and I want you to listen really carefully. There's a lot of history—I know there's a lot of history and I don't know what it is, and I have a hunch that oftentimes you don't see what's right in front of your nose, because it is all covered up with what you expect, because you almost did it right now. Are you with me?

MARGIE: Uh huh.

VIRGINIA: OK, now I'd like you to look at Casey and feel his skin through your hands at this moment and tell me what you feel. (Casey explodes into a smile.) (1983, pp. 112–114)

Virginia frequently used exaggeration to challenge overgeneralizations by making them appear ridiculous, and there are many examples in the transcript in this book.

There's a certain kind of thing that happens when you can bring things to the level of absurdity. Have you noticed that? It bypasses defenses, when you do it in a kind and loving way. (1984)

At other times she was more direct, saying skeptically, "Do you really believe that?" or "I don't believe it." She knew when overgeneralizations that interfered with family communication had to be challenged, and she did whatever was necessary to do it.

Specific Verbal Patterns for Gathering Information Gracefully

Virginia consistently talked in ways that allowed her to gather specific information about the interaction among family members. Although each verbal pattern in itself made a relatively small difference, taken together they had a powerful impact.

Virginia would often begin by speaking to the children about something seemingly inconsequential. In the transcript in *Satir Step by Step* she asks where everyone sits at the dinner table; this makes it easier to elicit the family's patterns of interaction innocuously. (1983, pp. 16–18) As she did this, she used specific questions to pinpoint what occurs in the family, asking "who, what, when, where, how, specifically?" and noticing any nonverbal responses that indicated communication patterns. Often she would go on to request a demonstration, so she could see and hear the behavior itself and know exactly what she had to work with.

After creating a sculpture depicting the pecking order among the children and verifying with both parents that it is accurate, Virginia turns to the mother and asks her to demonstrate how she deals with the children's fighting when her husband isn't there:

Now Margie, I'd like you to come and do what you do at home when this is happening. What do you try to do? (1983, p. 58)

After Margie describes and demonstrates what she does, Virginia asks the mother to sit down and turns to the father:

When you see this happen, would you come and show me what you do when this is going on? (1983, p. 62)

After the father shows what he does when the mother isn't there, Virginia asks how they respond when they are both present:

Now, when this happens and the two of you are here, Casey and Margie, I'd like to know what happens. When you're both present with the kids. (1983, p. 64)

Now Virginia has specific information about what each parent does separately and how this changes when they are both present, which also provides information about the marital relationship.

Virginia would also gather information by using a form of indirect question described by linguists as a *conversational postulate*. "Now, would you like to change anything about that?" (1983, p. 38) or "Is there something special you'd like to talk about, for you?" (1983, p. 40) The literal answer to such questions is yes or no. However, most people do not just answer such a question with a simple "yes," but spontaneously go on to provide the information indicated.

Virginia also used gentle statements that actually functioned as questions and are called *embedded questions*. "I was wondering if you knew anything about what it feels like to get angry." (1983, p. 38) "I wonder how you feel, Margie, about Casey's . . . at least his feeling that he's the bad guy?" (1983, p. 66) Since these statements don't require an answer, there is no demand for a response. However, most people respond by providing the information requested.

These and other easily learned linguistic patterns in Virginia's work are described in detail in her book *Changing with Families*, (1976) coauthored with Richard Bandler and John Grinder.

Although Virginia thought of herself as nurturing and supportive of family growth, she was persistent and direct (some would say confrontational) when going after information and feelings that she knew would be useful to the family. After the father, Casey, says, "Well it makes me the bad guy," the dialogue goes as follows:

VIRGINIA: Yeah, I wonder. Let's sit down for a minute, and I want to find out something else. That's what happens, but that's not what you like to happen, I gather. Now, I wonder how you feel, Margie, about Casey's . . . at least his feeling that he's the bad guy?

MARGIE: I don't think so. If he speaks up. I do discipline the children.

VIRGINIA: No, that's not what I'm asking you right now. I'm asking you how you *feel* about Casey feeling he's the bad guy.

MARGIE: Well, he does, very definitely.

VIRGINIA: And I'd like to know how you feel about his feeling that, dear.

MARGIE: I feel sad for Casey. (1983, p.66)

In this example, Virginia had to ask her question three times before she got an appropriate answer from Margie.

Specific Verbal Patterns for Helping People Change

Presuppositions

One way that Virginia brought about change was to state what she wanted a person to experience as a presupposition. Presuppositions include everything that is assumed to be true in a sentence, in contrast to what is directly stated.

One way to identify presuppositions in a sentence is to negate it, and notice what is still true. Take this simple sentence: "It's good that you're willing to express yourself." When we negate this sentence, we get: "It's not good that you're willing to express yourself." Despite the negation, "you're willing to express yourself" remains as true as it was in the first sentence.

People typically focus on what they can agree or disagree about, while ignoring what is presupposed. When listeners do not notice presuppositions, they are accepted, and the listener tends to act as if they are true. When someone accepts a new presupposition, he begins to respond to it, often without becoming consciously aware of having made a shift. If we make the statement above into a question—"Do you think it's good or bad that you're willing to express yourself?"—this focuses the listener's attention more strongly on whether the whole sentence is true, making the presuppositions even less noticeable.

Here are examples of Virginia delivering empowering presuppositions to the family within questions. The important presuppositions are noted in parentheses.

What is there for you, at this moment, Margie, that is some vulnerability in you that you know about, that you'd like your family to honor, maybe particularly Casey? (*There is some vulnerability, you know about it, and you'd like your family to honor it.*) (1983, p. 84)

Are you aware that the bad feelings come, and then comes the anger? (*You have bad feelings that come before anger.*) (1983, p. 100)

What can you do about that? (*You can do something.*) (1983, p. 128)

What was it you saw and heard right now that made you not believe? (*Not believing was a result of perceptions in the present.*) (1983, p. 130)

After delivering one or more instructions in the form of presuppositions, Virginia often asked, "How do you feel about that?" When asked about their feelings, most people have to pause to check and then search for words to describe them. This typically takes more concentration than answering other questions, which distracts people from noticing the presuppositions.

How willing are you to act on your wish right now and take the risk that one of you might get hurt? (*You are willing*

*to act on your wish right now, and take the risk that one of
you might get hurt.*) (1983, p. 106)

Now that you've gotten over the feeling of strangeness,
how does it feel to have her here? (*You have gotten over the
feeling of strangeness.*) (1983, p. 112)

Virginia hated manipulating people, but she used presuppositions systematically to empower people and to propel them into making their lives better. For more examples and more detailed discussion
of how presuppositions work, see Appendix I.

Embedded Commands

Traditional hypnosis uses many direct commands, such as "feel
relaxed," "sleep deeply," etc. Since direct commands are recognized
consciously, the person may consciously resist responding to them.

In contrast, Milton Erickson used *embedded commands*, commands that were placed in a longer sentence, with the embedded command marked out nonverbally by a shift in voice tone or volume, a
gesture, a glance, a tilt of the head, etc.

It's possible for a person to *feel relaxed.*

How enjoyable it is to *sleep deeply* and *dream pleasant
dreams.*

These are examples of "mixed state" communication. The listener consciously responds to the entire sentence, while not recognizing but unconsciously responding to the embedded command.
Such commands can be especially effective when the whole sentence
seems to be directed toward someone else.

Although embedded commands were an explicit part of Erickson's work, few therapists use them systematically, particularly in the
absence of a formal trance induction. Virginia, however, used them fully,
and such commands contributed significantly to her effectiveness.

While discussing the father's getting angry and yelling, Virginia
says to the son, "Some way—and you're saying that if he could *find*

some way to treat that differently—is that what you hope for?" (1983, p. 34) The italicized words are an embedded command directed at the father and marked by an increase in volume.

A couple of minutes later Virginia repeats this command. "OK, well, what I'm trying to get at here is that you're talking about how you think maybe *your daddy could do differently with his temper,* and I think we all have to struggle with that." (1983, p. 38) Virginia signals the command by facing down with her eyes closed while gesturing toward the father.

Soon after that, Virginia says, "You'd like to somehow have your *dad look at this a little differently*—what about you, for yourself?" (1983, p. 38) Virginia looks and gestures toward the father.

After hearing about a time when the mother was absent for two months and the father got on well with the kids, and after determining that the mother is comparing her husband's fathering to that of the mother's own idealized father, Virginia says to the mother:

"OK. What are the chances *now,* Margie, for *find*ing *out,* for you really *find*ing *out, how Casey would feel comfortable fathering his children? . . .* and seeing how far you could *let that happen?*" Virginia is looking intently at Margie, with her right hand on the side of her head and nodding her head.

MARGIE: I don't know how far. Children upset Casey.

VIRGINIA: We'll get into it some more, but, what I need to find out is, if you are willing to *go on a search to find out how Casey really wants to do his fathering.* You may not know it. (14, p. 76) (Virginia looks down with eyes closed; her voice becomes softer.)

Linkage

To make it easier for people to do what she asked, and to avoid objections, Virginia would sometimes begin by asking the person to do something that most people find simple and completely acceptable, such as "Look at me," "Close your eyes," or "Step closer." This simple instruction was followed by "and," and then by the task that Virginia wanted them to do. Starting with a simple task implied that the next task would be just as easy to do.

I want you to look at mc now, and I want you to listen
really carefully. (1983, p.112)

OK, now I'd like you to look at Casey and feel his skin
through your hands at this moment and tell me what you feel.
(Casey explodes into a smile.) (1983, p. 114)

All right. Now. Will you look at Casey and will you say
it to him, because this is a new step, I gather, if at this moment you feel you're criticizable. (1983, p. 130)

Although implications are weaker than presuppositions, they
also make it easier for people to try out new perceptions and behaviors. Virginia used implications as widely as she used presuppositions.
When Coby says, "I wish I was older," Virginia replies, "You wish you
were older. Well, I can't do much about that!" and laughs. (1983,
pp. 38-40) The implication is that she can do a lot about other things.

Specific Use of Generalities

Many therapists are just vague. Virginia, however, used general
statements in a directed way to bring about change. Right at the start
of the session in *Satir Step by Step* Virginia says:

How about Casey and Margie and Lucy and Lisa and
Coby and Betty . . . . I remembered! Susie . . . . Oh, I missed
one. Come on up—any chair you like—and we can move it
around. Nothing's in concrete. (1983, p.16)

Virginia's statement that "nothing's in concrete" means "anything can be changed," and clearly refers to the seating arrangement.
However, because she says it as a generalization—what linguists call
a "non-referring noun phrase"—it also functions as a statement about
the family and its communication. Statements like this prepare family
members to think that change is possible and that they can have the
kind of lives they want.

After she identified some of the family's sensitive issues, Virginia
would talk about them in general terms, using pronouns like "people," the universal "we," "those things," "something," etc. An example
is her response to the family's concerns about anger. Virginia says:

You know that whenever we get mad it's hard to see anyhow. (1983, p. 22) You were mad. Well, those things happen sometimes. (1983, p. 26) I think we all have to struggle with that. (1983, p. 38) We learn from whatever our experiences are. OK? It's not because it is bad, it's just that we learn certain things. (1983, p. 82)

And in a funny way I have a hunch that when people don't know how to say what they want, and don't know what to do to get it, fighting is the easiest way. See, I think if we don't know how to do what we really want and we do know how to fight, that does help us a little, but the pains are great in it. (1983, p. 94)

Even when the context indicated what she was referring to, Virginia discussed difficult issues in a general way without tackling them directly with the person who brought them up. She then redefined, reframed, taught general principles, or joked about trivial examples—all without directly engaging the person who had the problem, and without putting him "on the spot." Using this technique early in the session allowed her to build a foundation for change. Later she could tackle the problem directly with the people involved, knowing that she had already made changes that cleared the way for completing the work. Since Virginia had connected humor with the general statements and examples, it was also easier to bring people back to humor if they got stuck in being too serious.

The only way a person can understand a general statement is for him to search through his own experiences to find those that fit. If a statement is broad enough, nearly any experience in the overall category can fit. General statements invited all family members—as well as the audience or observers when Virginia taught publicly—to consider their own experiences with the same issue. So while Virginia might have appeared to be intervening with only one family member, she was actually working with all other members and anyone else within earshot. Since everyone in the family was invited to make internal changes with the same issue, they often came to shared understandings that brought them closer together.

Virginia's style of redescribing a problem in a general way made it easy for observers to be drawn into working with their own similar personal issues and experiences. This aspect of her work made it particularly difficult for those studying her to remain detached enough to notice exactly what she did, and how she did it so precisely.

Temporal Predicate Shifts

Virginia was adept at using the perception of time to facilitate change. Every sentence has a verb, and verbs indicate past, present, or future. Using past tense tends to dissociate and separate the person from an event or behavior, while present tense associates the person into it. Describing a problem behavior in past tense indicates that it is behavior that belongs in the past, leaving room for new behavior in the present. We can begin by describing a possible new behavior in future tense, and then shift to present tense, thus presupposing that the behavior has already been achieved. By describing past events and then shifting to present consequences, it's possible to build new and more useful beliefs about causes and effects.

These temporal predicate shifts can be powerful tools in changing people's responses, particularly when they are combined with presuppositions. Although I could find no examples of her use of temporal predicate shifts in the 1974 transcript in *Satir Step by Step*, there are many examples from the 1986 transcript in this book. This may indicate that she added this to her work at some time in the intervening years. For a more detailed description of temporal predicate shifts, see Appendix I of this book, or Chapter 2, "Utilizing Time," in *Change Your Mind and Keep the Change* (1987).

Distinction Between Perception and Reality: "Model of the World"

Virginia clearly understood that her main focus of change was people's images or *perceptions* of their world. When perceptions change, people's beliefs, responses and behaviors change as well. Once people's perceptions and feelings are different, it's relatively easy to teach more effective ways to communicate.

When a family has difficulties, it's often because family members believe that the world is a certain way. This belief is not useful because it presupposes that it is a reality that can't be changed. Often Virginia would listen to what a family member would say and then restate it as a *perception*. The distinction between how things *are* and how they *seem,* or how someone *sees* things or *thinks* they are, is subtle, but it opens the door to other possible ways of seeing the same events. Words or phrases indicating perceptions are italicized in the examples below.

> You'd like to somehow have your dad *look* at this a little differently. (1983, p. 38)

> What happened that Susie got her hands on your hair? What's your *idea* about that? (1983, p. 42)

> Everybody's got their own *picture,* so we'll see. (1983, p. 50)

COBY: Well, yes, ma'am, but you know, he loses his temper too easy.

VIRGINIA: I see. So sometimes you *think* your father *thinks* you do something, and then you don't do it, and then you don't know how to *tell* him or he doesn't *hear* you, or something like that? Is that what you're saying? (1983, pp. 34-36)

Virginia also modeled the distinction between perception and reality in her own behavior as she told the family her understanding of its situation.

> OK. Let me show you a picture that I see at the moment. I just want to get the picture out, and then you help me to check it and that. And I think it starts out, Coby—and this is my picture in my head from what I learned, and it may not fit at all, but it could. (1983, p. 54)

The elements mentioned in this section are often described as components of hypnotic communication. Virginia generally had harsh words for hypnosis, because she disliked the idea of manipulating people. However, this type of hypnotic communication was an important part of her work. This was most apparent in the "processes" or "meditations" that she used with large groups. In these processes, she asked people to close their eyes and relax, and then took them on a carefully structured and overtly hypnotic journey. For an example of one of Virginia's hypnotic meditations, see Appendix IV.

Virginia also used many other patterns of hypnotic communication, both verbal and nonverbal. For more detail about these, see *TRANCE-*

formations (1981), or *The Patterns of the Hypnotic Techniques of Milton H. Erickson, Vol. I* (1975), both by Bandler and Grinder.

Physical Contact

One of the most obvious hallmarks of Virginia's work was her use of touch. Although it is perhaps the most controversial aspect of her work (any physical contact between therapist and client is still expressly prohibited as unethical in mainstream psychiatry), she felt it was crucial. Touch is an essential part of family intimacy. Studies have shown that without it, infants who are otherwise well cared for will die. Yet troubled families typically either don't touch at all, or only touch roughly when angry or frustrated, or during sex.

In addition to its essential role in intimacy, touch has a way of getting a person's attention more effectively than sounds or sights, and attention is essential for learning. Virginia insisted on using touch to amplify any important positive communication or new learning and thus to consolidate change. Previous sections include several examples of this.

Virginia sometimes began by making physical contact with the children, who are typically more open to this than adults. Soon she was literally reaching out to all family members. Anyone who experienced Virginia's touch will tell you that it was simple, direct, and felt completely natural. She probably did more touching in one session than most therapists do in a year, creating positive connections among family members where loving touch had been lost altogether or had been replaced by roughness and violence.

In her videotape "Of Rocks and Flowers" (1983), Virginia works with a blended family with a history of severe physical abuse on both sides. In a moving segment in which she interacts only with the two young children, she has them touch her face gently, reciprocates, and then asks them if they would like to do the same with their parents. Then she brings the parents back in and patiently coaches both the children and the parents, suggesting that the children initiate this kind of contact several times a day.

Then she demonstrates with both parents the difference between grabbing roughly in anger and holding firmly yet protectively when they want to stop the children from doing something. She continues until both parents show *behaviorally* that they know how to do this. For those who would like to study exactly how she did this, a verbatim transcript of this session appears in Appendix II; viewing the videotape is even better.

Following this session, in an interview with Ramon Corrales of the Family Therapy Institute of Kansas City, Virginia commented on her touching:

> There had been so many things happening, and the fear was so strong in relation to these children that if you thought of one image it was like they were monsters. So one of the things that I wanted to do was also to see that they had the capacity to respond with a touch, using myself in that regard by having them put their hands on my face—that it was a kind of a mirror for the family itself, the people in the family. And then allowing them and encouraging them to do that with their own parents. See, touch, that comes out of that kind of ambiance which was there at the time, says things that no words can say. And that whole part of where there was the gentleness, that, too, is part of the whole thing.
>
> Now, for me, my touch is not going to send much to you unless I am integrated myself, unless I really feel whole myself: then energy moves out. If I feel I *have* to touch, or have to be careful about touching . . . that won't work. Because it's not a gimmick, and it's not a strategy. It's a living kind of passing back and forth of energy. Now, when that condition is there, then I know that one touch with energy passing back and forth—a real feeling of one human being really touching another in a literal sense—is probably worth hours and hours of something that doesn't contain that.
>
> You know about throwing the baby out with the bath water? Well, some touch is used for sex purposes and aggression purposes. And so many people have thrown touch out because it got used for those purposes, instead of saying, "OK. That's not the touch we want." No more than we want to come out blaming in such a way. We don't throw out our words because we don't want to use them for blaming; we find dif-

ferent words. And I frankly have to say that *if I couldn't have the energy that comes out with touch, I am certain I could not have the kind of really good results that I have.*

These are most of the larger patterns that made Virginia's work so effective, and all of them are evident in the verbatim transcript that follows. Each of these patterns could be divided into smaller pieces and described in more detail, and there are also many other supporting nonverbal elements. I invite readers to identify additional patterns by studying the videotape and transcript, to continue to amplify our understanding of Virginia's work.

Virginia's more subtle nonverbal perceptions and behaviors are harder to write about—her timing, her intonation patterns, the nonverbal cues she used to know how a family member was responding to a particular intervention, etc. Many of these smaller elements can only be learned by studying the videotape and by doing what Virginia herself did: closely observing how family members responded to each other and to her interventions—keeping those that worked and discarding those that didn't.

At the beginning of the weekend workshop from which the transcript in this book is taken, Virginia described her reasons for being there:

I'm aware that this is a very important occasion. And the importance of this occasion is that we are putting into an image form something that I believe will be very helpful to people. You know for years we've been talking to people, we've been writing books. You know, with all the books that have been written and all the words that have been given to people, wouldn't you think that we would have improved more?

It seems that we have to have something else to learn about ourselves. When video came in, I didn't know the power of it right away. But I've begun to see how very powerful it is, and that images are probably more important than anything else. To be able to see something is a very important part of making a new possibility. (1989)

I proceed from the theory that my therapeutic job is to expand, redirect, and reshape individuals' ways of coping with each other and themselves, so they can solve their own problems in more healthy and relevant ways. Problems are not the problem; coping is the problem. Coping is the outcome of self-worth, rules of the family systems, and links to the outside world.

—VIRGINIA SATIR (1983, p. 156)

"Forgiving Parents"

In march 1986, Virginia Satir met with about 30 therapists and educators for the purpose of creating a videotaped record of
her therapeutic work. She spent two days with the group in a television
studio, demonstrating and describing a variety of the ways in which
she worked with family members. This entire weekend workshop is
available as a set of seven videotapes totaling over eight hours (1989).

Late in the morning of the first day, Virginia asked people to
share their responses to what she had just demonstrated about family
dynamics and communication during the previous two hours. Linda,
39, came up and described how she had been strongly moved by
Virginia's work. "I'm getting this tremendous sense of the profound
connection that I could have with people," she said. Linda went on to
describe her conflict between feeling "incredibly powerful" in connecting with people and "feeling very very sad about the distance I
feel from people so often."

Simply stated, Linda's desire was to be able to connect with people,
but she was ambivalent about doing it. Virginia accepted this outcome
and devoted the entire session to achieving it. As she began to explore
this ambivalence, Linda soon revealed a great resentment for her mother.
Virginia then began a process that led to Linda's feeling compassion,
love, and forgiveness for her mother instead of resentment.

Since Linda could now feel compassion and forgiveness for the "arch-villain" of her childhood, connecting with other people would be easy. A followup interview with Linda three years later details the lasting impact that this session had on her communication with her mother, and her ability to connect with others.

This session is a particularly rich example of Virginia's work. It is available as the third tape, "Forgiving Parents," in the Satir video-tape series "Family Relations" (1989). At the end of this session Virginia says, "I have spoken to you about the fact that I have been working with families for over forty years, and I see a lot of things. Everything I strive for, you just saw."

The transcript of this session is presented here for those who would like to study Virginia's work carefully. The transcript is essentially verbatim; only some small repetitions and "ums" have been omitted for clarity. Since the transcript is verbatim, some of the sentences look a bit strange in print. However, presenting the exact words that Virginia spoke allows people to know that it is an accurate record of what occurred.

All material within parentheses is either a description of non-verbal behavior or a commentary about what is happening. Although it is impossible to convey all the detail of the nonverbal interaction that is available on the videotape—position, posture, gestures, expressions, fleeting smiles and glances, timing, tone, volume and tempo shifts, etc.—enough description has been added so that readers can follow the overall flow of events without having seen the videotape.

The commentary describing or explaining Virginia's work or Linda's responses appears in parentheses and *italics*. Brackets are used for brief descriptions that identify specific patterns such as [meaning reframing] that were discussed in the preceding chapter. Those who wish to read the verbatim transcript alone can skip this commentary.

The number at the beginning of each paragraph shows the time, in minutes and seconds, from the beginning of the session—both to provide a measure of how long each segment took, and as a convenient way to refer to transcript segments in the commentary.

The Transcript

00:00   VIRGINIA: I'd like to hear now from some other people here about what happened for you, again, ah, with this last section. Who is somebody who would like to share with me about that—what happened for you?

00:11   LINDA: I'll share.

00:12   VIRGINIA: Come. (Virginia reaches out her right hand, and Linda walks up from the group and takes Virginia's hand with her left.) Thank you. And you are—?

00:20   LINDA: I'm Linda.

00:21   VIRGINIA: Linda. Hi, Linda.

00:22   LINDA: Hi. This whole thing has been a very emotional experience today (gesturing to her right with her right hand). And I think what has come up for me is that I started getting this tremendous sense of the profound connection that I could have with people. And I am somewhere in between being incredibly powerful (gesturing to her right with her right hand) and a total wimp (gesturing to her left). (Linda laughs easily and the group laughs with her. Linda continues to smile.)

(Linda has stated a clear sequential conflict or polarity between two extremes: "incredibly powerful" and "total wimp." She has also demonstrated with her hand gestures that she experiences this polarity as sorted in space: "power" is on her right, while "wimp" is on her left.)

00:50   VIRGINIA: OK, I have a picture for that. (*Virginia's response is very specific. She doesn't just say, "I understand"; she is explicit that she has a visual picture of what Linda said.*) We'll go ahead; yes. (As Virginia says this, she looks up to her left for a remembered visual image. See Appendix III. *"We'll go ahead" presupposes it's possible to go ahead.* Then she speaks to the group while gesturing toward Linda with her left hand)

00:53   VIRGINIA: Does anybody know about that, the feeling of being "I can do it in the world" (gesturing powerfully with her left hand) and then "Oh, no, I'm a piece of wet spaghetti"? (Virginia allows her whole body to crumple and wilt momentarily.) How many know that one? Let's see how many know that? (Virginia raises her hand and people in the group raise their hands in acknowledgement.) Oh, wonderful! OK.

(This is a nice example of what some people have called "normalization." Virginia points out that Linda's conflict is a problem that everyone—including Virginia—experiences, and therefore it's "normal." When people regard a problem as normal, it appears easier to resolve. By acknowledging that she has experienced the same problem, Virginia establishes a relationship among equals.)

(At the same time she is doing something else very important. By explicitly asking group members to search through their experiences for ones similar to what Linda experiences, she is inviting them to participate in Linda's therapeutic journey by identifying with her [switch referential index]. Those who accept this invitation will experience many of the same, or similar, therapeutic changes that Linda does.)

01:02   LINDA: Only today I was much closer to the powerfulness, (gesturing again to her right) and feeling, um—I was weeping back there (Linda laughs briefly, almost crying, gesturing toward where she had been sitting in the group) for the first section, just feeling, um (gesturing toward her chest) very, very sad about the distance that I feel from people so often, and yet the other part of me wanting to just—and at times I am in touch with this—where I can just embrace *everyone* (gesturing with her right hand) and I feel total love for everyone. And I feel like I could be instrumental in helping people change, and I was looking at you and how beautifully you do this . . . and wanting to do it, too, and whatever it means for me.

(Linda has restated her ambivalence in more detail: "powerful" means to connect with people, embracing and loving them, while "wimp" means feeling distance from them. Linda wants to be able to connect with people, and this is the outcome Virginia seeks and works toward throughout the session.)

01:43   VIRGINIA (nodding):   Wonderful, Linda. (Virginia brings up Linda's hand and pats it with her other hand. *"Wonderful"* is a non-specific positive acknowledgment of Linda. Notice that she *doesn't respond to the negative side and offer sympathy: "It's too bad you can't feel connected." Instead she amplifies the positive side and says "wonderful." And indeed it is wonderful that Linda has a goal for herself, that she has expressed it, etc.)* Let me just do a little something with you. (*"Let me just do a little something with you" asks Linda to consent to whatever Virginia decides to do with her. Virginia then looks down left, listening to her internal voice. See Appendix III.*) Can you see a place in your life to be "wet spaghetti?"

(So far, Linda has described "wet spaghetti" as bad. Virginia asks Linda to think of a context in which "wet spaghetti" could be good [context reframing] in order to broaden the way Linda thinks of this part of her polarity. Rather than bluntly ordering her to think of this context, she uses a gentler form: "Can you see a place in your life to be 'wet spaghetti?'" [conversational postulate], which is also an instruction [embedded command] to see a visual image of this context.)

01:53   LINDA: To *be* "wet spaghetti?"

01:55   VIRGINIA: Umhum hm hm hm. (Virginia lets her body crumple and wilt again.) Yeah.

01:57   LINDA: Yeah, I think I can.

01:58   VIRGINIA: All right, what I'd like you to do is now look at that picture (*Virginia not only explicitly says, "Look at that picture," she also looks and gestures upward, where people most easily visualize. See Appendix III.* Linda also looks upward) and seeing yourself as "wet spaghetti," and let's see what comes out of that for you. (*As Virginia finishes the sentence, she looks down to her left, listening to her internal voice.*)

02:06   VIRGINIA: Because I got a little worried at first that you were going to get rid of that "wet spaghetti" thing. (Linda laughs briefly.) And then I thought you would be right back where you got before: you would be "skinny" (*Virginia often used the word "skinny" to mean limited, narrow, or one-sided*) in one little old thing that you could do, and that is always be powerful. (Virginia straightens up to look powerful.)

(The two preceding sentences are not the clearest Virginia ever spoke. She wants Linda to acknowledge the value—at least in cer-

tain contexts—of being "wet spaghetti," so that she can value the part of her she has called "wimp." Valuing both sides of a polarity is an important first step in healing inner conflict. Most of us, like Linda, start by thinking that one side is good and the other bad. Virginia uses past tense to talk about wanting to get rid of this part, placing this thinking in Linda's past and making it easier for Linda to be open to valuing this part in the present.)

02:18   VIRGINIA: But let me see now about the "wet spaghetti."

02:22   LINDA: OK.

02:24   VIRGINIA: When can you see that just being "Yumnum"? (Virginia looks up and smacks her lips with delight. *She specifically asks Linda to visualize by using "see." By using the word "when," she presupposes that there is a time and place where being "wet spaghetti" would be yummy.)*

02:26   LINDA: I see myself maybe lying on my couch with a bunch of friends, just feeling totally vulnerable (Linda gestures in a relaxed way and touches her chest.) and having people nurture and take care of me. (Linda gestures toward Virginia.)

02:35   VIRGINIA: OK. How does that feel?

02:38   LINDA (smiling broadly):   I . . . I like it.

02:40   VIRGINIA: That's good. (The group laughs.) Now, that would *not* be the way you would [want to] be if you wanted to carry a big bag of groceries, would it? (*Having got a full, positive response from Linda, Virginia immediately points out that while this is appropriate to this context, it is not appropriate to others.* [context reframing])

02:47   LINDA: No.

02:48   VIRGINIA: No. All right, so what does this lead us to? This leads us *to choice . . . to choice.* (*"To choice" is an embedded command to Linda that this understanding gives her choice.*) That when I need to do this (gesturing in front of her), I can pull this out of me. When I need to do this (gesturing to her left), I can pull this out of me. But if I've got a rule I always have to be a certain way, then I can't do it. (Linda nods.)

03:04 VIRGINIA: Now I also want to ask you another question. Do you really think you can love everybody at the same time? (*Now Virginia directs Linda's attention to the other side of the polarity by questioning the universal statement that she made earlier: "I can embrace everyone and I feel total love for everyone." By adding "at the same time," Virginia makes Linda's statement even more extreme. She is following up on the rule idea she just mentioned [3:00]. If I think I always have to love everyone, this will be hard to accomplish, and it could lead to failure and probably also self-criticism. If my goal includes flexibility and choice, it will be more possible to reach it, and more satisfying.*)

03:11 LINDA: At the same time?

03:13 VIRGINIA: Yeah, or can you love everybody, period? (Virginia looks and gestures up to her left. *This is a nonverbal invitation for Linda to search through her remembered images.*)

03:17 LINDA (*looking up to her right, where most people construct images of future possibilities*): I think that I can—I would like (touching her chest) to get to a place where I can go beyond people's personalities (gesturing in front of her, palm inward), which may be ugly at a given moment (gesturing in front of her, palm outward) and just love them (gesturing alternately toward her chest and Virginia's chest, *another nonverbal achnowledgement that Linda feels a close connection with Virginia*) for the connection that we might have as human beings, or that "light" that you were referring to (earlier in the day) or something. (*Linda is making a distinction that can be useful and therapeutic—between a person's behavior, which may be unpleasant, and his inner being. This is a distinction that Virginia made earlier in the workshop. Virginia acknowledges this, and goes on to ask how Linda will cope with the unpleasant behavior.*)

03:31 VIRGINIA: All right, what are you going to do with their nasty behavior?

03:34 LINDA: Well, I won't spend a lot of *time* around them. I'll make the choice of not hanging out with people that are nasty, but still I don't want to have *hate* for them. I want to love them for being human beings.

03:46   VIRGINIA: This is such a central thing, and I want to elaborate it a little bit. Um . . . (Virginia looks out at the group and then beckons to a man in the group, Randy, who happens to be a good friend of Linda's.)

03:53   LINDA (smiling):   Oh good! I'm *glad* you picked him. (The group laughs.)

03:56   VIRGINIA (jokingly, as Randy comes up to stand at Virginia's left side):   Well, I was reading your mind, you know, reading your mind. Don't believe it; I wasn't reading your mind. (*By saying she was reading Linda's mind and then saying she wasn't, Virginia is making a joke that keeps the atmosphere light. She playfully puts herself in the "expert/guru" role, and then quickly and explicitly steps out of it. By mentioning it, she is also leaving Linda with the possibility that she can read her mind. Denying it doesn't necessarily mean it isn't true, and people love to find explanations for coincidence.* Virginia next puts her left hand on Randy's shoulder briefly, while still talking to Linda.) OK. Now, what I heard you say is, "I don't want to go around with hate feelings." (*Virginia restates what Linda has said, both in order to get Linda's confirmation and to get her commitment to the statement before going on to utilize it.*)

04:07   LINDA: Right.

04:08   VIRGINIA: "I don't want to go around with hate feelings." (*By repeating the sentence, Virginia re-emphasizes what Linda has committed herself to. There's a cliche that says, "If you repeat something often enough, it becomes true," and Virginia often used repetition for emphasis.*) Now what you didn't say, but maybe *it's true,* is that *you know hate erodes you.* (Virginia gestures toward her stomach. *She is using "you" in a universal sense: "all of us." Virginia presupposes that hate erodes you; the only question is whether Linda knows it. "It's true" and "You know hate erodes you" are also embedded commands marked out by volume emphasis.*)

04:14   LINDA: Umhm.

04:15   VIRGINIA: Because what hate does is it starts eating on you. How many of you know that? (*By saying "What hate does . . . " and "How many of you know that," Virginia again presupposes that hate eats on you, and again achieves normalization, equality, and participation of the audience.*) It starts eating on you. And it eats and it eats, and the more you hate, the more you want to kill the object of the hate. (*By repeating that hate eats on you—three times—she is further emphasizing the truth of this statement* [repetition].) See, this runs a very interesting thing. Once you do a categorization, or you stereotype something, or you make a prejudicial kind of thing, then that has to be the focus of hate. It has to be the focus of—especially the prejudice bit—has to be a focus of hate [repetition].

04:45   VIRGINIA: Now, hate comes because you feel vulnerable. (*Virginia turns to Randy.*) Because if you weren't doing what you're doing—wearing that mustache, for instance. (turning back to Linda) You know, all mustached men have got very bad ideas in their minds. (*Linda and the group laugh; Randy smiles.*) That's what a lot of people say.

(*Virginia has been describing Linda's situation in terms of universal human processes, using non-referring noun phrases: "Hate erodes you," "The more you hate, the more you want to kill the object of hate," and "Hate comes because you feel vulnerable." After emphasizing the basic issues of vulnerability, hate, and killing, Virginia uses a trivial and ridiculous example—"You know, all mustached men have got very bad ideas in their mind"—to maintain lightness and humor while moving toward introducing Linda to new ways of thinking about the big issues. Virginia selects an example— "all mustached men . . . " where everyone will recognize that the hate is inappropriate. This builds a foundation for later challenging Linda's hateful feelings toward others as also being inappropriate.*)

04:59   VIRGINIA: Anyway, so there comes the fear. And the hate is to cover up the impotence. (*Virginia continues to speak in universal terms: "the fear," "the hate," "the impotence"—in contrast to "your fear," etc. This lets her make important points without confronting Linda directly.*) And so when we put ourselves in the spot of where we have to feel impotent, we start to erode ourselves. We start to erode [repetition]. (*Virginia's phrasing—"we erode ourselves"— presupposes that we are both the creators and the victims of hate. And since we do it to ourselves, we have the potential to change. This creates a different mind-set than describing it as "We hate others" or "Others did something awful to us." In the previous two sentences*

Virginia also shifts to the universal "we." This makes it gentler when she next turns to Linda and shifts to "you.")

05:16   VIRGINIA: All right. Now, you don't want to do that. Now, let us, for a moment now—we'll give him (gesturing over her shoulder toward Randy) some names later. (*"We'll give him some names later"* [non-referring noun phrase] *invites Linda to consider who in her life she is prejudiced toward. What names will Randy be given later? "Give him some names later" is also an embedded command, and indicates clearly that Virginia has a definite advance plan for what she will do later with Linda: deal with her prejudice toward someone in her family of origin.*) Think about what you want to do is keep yourself in as much congruence as possible, which is that you are letting yourself know what you feel.

05:31   LINDA: Umhm.

05:32   VIRGINIA: Now, actually the way out of hate is to let yourself know you're vulnerable, and that you are feeling impotent. (*Virginia doesn't ask, "Do you feel vulnerable when you feel hate?" She presupposes vulnerability—it's only a matter of whether you let yourself know about these feelings.*) That's a way out of hate.

05:40   VIRGINIA: When I work, I do something regularly in San Francisco with the people who work under the streets in the sewers and all kinds of places like that, and they are many people of different colored skins, and there's *much* trouble with those people. So what I do is I help them to develop and to discover their vulnerabilities—their fear of being loved, their fears—whatever they might be. (*By talking about "those people"* [non-referring noun phrase] *Virginia again gracefully discusses the issues at a universal level before turning back to deal directly with Linda.*) And so the first step in dealing with the hate (Virginia turns to Linda and takes both her hands in hers) is to allow yourself to be in touch with your own vulnerability.

06:07   VIRGINIA: Now, to *not* be in touch with your vulnerability *before*, you felt was a protection. It's this awful one over here—that mustache, you know, hides a lot of awful things. (*Most people believe they can protect themselves by not showing their vulnerability. Virginia attempts to put this into Linda's past by saying "before, you felt was a protection," and then shifts to present tense to describe the ridiculous example of mustached men* [temporal predicate shift]. *The implicit message is, "You used to believe this; now it's ridiculous.")*

06:15 LINDA: Well, it saved me. (*Linda also uses past tense—"saved." While she is saying her protection was important, she is leaving it in the past.*)

06:16 VIRGINIA (momentarily caught off balance by Linda's apparent disagreement):   Well, in a way yes, but not yet, in a way. (*By saying "but not yet, in a way," Virginia is presupposing that it didn't save Linda, but that she can be saved in the future.*) You misunderstood it, but that's all right. (*Linda's apparent disagreement with what Virginia said is labeled as a "misunderstanding"* [meaning reframing]. *Then Virginia accepts Linda's statement and goes on to explore what she means by it.*) "It saved you." OK. All right, so then here you are. (*Virginia looks down to her left for an auditory memory.*) And you said something about saving. What hate did you use to save you? (*Virginia begins to gather information to resolve the apparent misunderstanding.*)

06:37 LINDA: I didn't mean that the hate saved me. I meant protecting myself from being vulnerable saved me from what I perceived as things that would harm me—in my family, let's say.

06:50 VIRGINIA: All right. Now let's hold that a minute, (*"Hold that a minute" presupposes that after a minute, if Linda no longer holds what she's thinking, it will be gone.*) because now you are talking about something else. You are talking about your ability to *see* those things that would be harmful, and for you to then move away or beyond, or cope differently with it. That's a different thing, because that opens you up to allowing yourself a whole lot of possibilities. I don't want—what I want on this concept is to be able to help people to see clearly that they always have choices. (*Although Virginia is speaking of "people"* [non-referring noun phrase] *she clearly means Linda. This is a way of normalizing and of bringing the group along with her work with Linda. Virginia also changes the description in a way that opens up choice. "Not being vulnerable" becomes "seeing danger and coping with it." In fact, coping with danger could include being vulnerable.*)

07:22 LINDA: Umhm.

07:23   VIRGINIA: So let's make—who was the—let's see who in your family—father? Mother? Who was it that you—or both or how? (*Virginia follows up on Linda's comment about "things that would harm me—in my family, let's say" [6:46]. Virginia starts listing principal family members while watching for Linda's response. But Virginia is not very clear, so Linda's response is confusion. She doesn't respond directly to Virginia's mentioning father and mother.*)

07:31   LINDA: That I what?

07:32   VIRGINIA: When you grew up, that you wanted to protect yourself against?

07:34   LINDA (emphatically):   *Mother.* (Linda closes her eyes and averts her head briefly.)

07:35   VIRGINIA (to Randy):   All right, well you are the wrong sex for that, but stay up here. (Linda laughs.) Let's pick up somebody. (Virginia beckons to an older woman in the group.) Would you come and be the mother? (The woman from the group walks up and takes Randy's place.)

07:42   LINDA (laughing): Oh, what have I gotten myself into?

07:45   VIRGINIA (lightheartedly):   Well, I can tell you that whenever you get into something with me, what people report is that it ends *wonderfully*. (*The group laughs. By using the general terms "people" and "wonderfully," Virginia paints an inviting picture, yet without promising anything specific to Linda.*)

07:50   LINDA: OK.

07:51   VIRGINIA: So I will tell you that, and I know that's true. All right, now, I already have a picture, but I would like you to tell me how come, or what is the picture of *her* (gesturing toward the woman playing Linda's mother) that makes you feel vulnerable? (*Notice that Virginia says "what is the picture of her"—in contrast to "what does she do," for instance—deliberately referring to Linda's image of her mother, rather than to her mother [model of the world]. Virginia also prefaces this with the parallel statement, "I have a picture" of what Linda is saying.*)

08:06   LINDA: I'm supposed to be picturing her as my mother?

08:08   VIRGINIA: Yes, that's right. And give her—

08:10   LINDA: She . . . um—

08:11   VIRGINIA: Say "you" to her. It will help. (*By using "she," Linda can remain distant from her image of her mother, with little emotion. Using "you" will tend to put her back into the problem interaction and to re-engage her feelings more fully* [association].)

08:12   LINDA (resentfully):   OK. You, you . . . You cannot stand my joyfulness, and so you are constantly putting me down and picking on me. (Linda gestures repeatedly with her palm up in a hitting motion toward her mother.)

08:21   VIRGINIA: All right, now tell her—(Virginia looks up and to the left for remembered images.) Let's have some dialogue, how does she pick on you? (*This is a first invitation for Linda to take her mother's place* [shift referential index] *by taking on her mother's external behavior. Hearing her mother's specific words will engage Linda more fully. At the same time it will give Virginia specific information about exactly what Linda's mother says and how she says it.*)

08:24   LINDA (critically):   You're too skinny! (*Linda is taking on her mother's critical behavior, becoming her through role-playing* [shift referential index].)

08:26   VIRGINIA (lightly, looking up and left):   Oh, "too skinny." That's wonderful. (Linda smiles.) That's a wonderful one. (*By using the word "wonderful" twice, and a light tone of voice for something that Linda has thought of as serious and awful, Virginia keeps Linda in a more positive state from which she can see her mother more objectively.*) Is she heavy?

(*Fritz Perls used to say that "Contact is the appreciation of differences"—in contrast to seeing differences as bad. By asking if her mother is heavy, Virginia brings out a possible difference between Linda and her mother, and puts the comment "You're too skinny" into the context of this difference* [context reframing].)

08:30   LINDA: Chunky.

08:31   VIRGINIA: Chunky (joking, looking up and left). OK. All right. Well, I understand that one. (Both Linda and the group laugh. *With this short joking comment Virginia accomplishes several things. First, the joke further lightens Linda's state. Problems are more easily solved when you can laugh at them. Second, this comment essentially says, "I'm like your mother," another example of Virginia's stance of equality with people she works with.)*

(Perhaps most important, this comment will begin to change Linda's feelings toward her mother. Linda has just expressed her anger toward, and distance from, her mother. Previously she expressed her deep connection and respect for Virginia. These are the two opposite feelings that Linda expressed sequentially when she first described her conflict [00:22 and 01:02]. By creating an identity between Virginia and Linda's mother, even in this small and joking way, these two opposite feelings will begin to exist simultaneously, rather than sequentially, and will start to blend together and resolve.)

08:34   VIRGINIA: All right, now what else does she say?

08:37   LINDA: She used—You always tell me that I talk too loud, and to calm down and keep it down. (Linda gestures with a pushing-down motion. *Linda begins by describing what her mother does, and then shifts to role-playing.*)

08:43   VIRGINIA: All right, OK. You do that. "You talk too loud and you should keep it down." (Virginia looks up and left briefly and then looks down and left, recalling what Linda said earlier.) What else? "You are too skinny; you should talk softer." She doesn't tell you that, though. [She says] "Keep your voice down."

08:55   LINDA: "Why don't you do something with your talent? You are so talented; you never do anything with your talent." (*This time Linda completely puts herself into her mother's role.*)

08:58   VIRGINIA: What talents is she thinking about? Are they the same as you think—(*Virginia starts to draw a parallel between Linda and her mother, but Linda interrupts her. Virginia returns to this systematically later [24:16].*)

09:00   LINDA: Music.

09:01   VIRGINIA (lightly):   All right, you're not—You're wasting your talent, eh?

09:03   LINDA: Right.

09:04   VIRGINIA: Oh, OK. (Linda smiles and the group laughs.) What else?

09:06   LINDA (laughing):   That's not enough?

09:09   VIRGINIA: Well, as long as we're starting on this string, why don't we make a *big* one out of it? (*Virginia is deliberately emphasizing and exaggerating Linda's complaints with a light and joking tone of voice. This begins to make the complaints seem humorous, which will make it easier for Linda to examine and, later, change them.*)

09:14   LINDA: OK. Um, "You're just like your father."

09:16   VIRGINIA (lightly, looking up and left):   Oh wonderful. That's a great one. (*Virginia keeps the humor going by saying, "Oh wonderful," and "That's a great one."* Linda laughs.) Now, what's wrong with your father that you are like him?

09:20   LINDA: He's Irish.

09:21   VIRGINIA: Oh, I see. Oh, so and you are *half* Irish.

09:24   LINDA: Right.

09:25   VIRGINIA (joking):   So tell her that she can only be *half* critical of you; because one half is her. (Linda laughs. *Virginia continues joking to lighten Linda's seriousness and to help her move to a new, more objective perspective* [dissociation]. *Virginia uses the logic implicit in "You're like your father and he's Irish" to point out that since she's only half Irish, her mother can only be half critical .*) But nevertheless, OK. (softly) But what else about your father?

09:32   LINDA: Ah, irresponsible.

09:35   VIRGINIA: Does that mean that he doesn't give her the money she wants, or he doesn't consult her or . . . ? (*"Irresponsible" is both judgmental and general. Virginia asks Linda to be more specific by giving her several possibilities that are descriptive rather than judgmental.*)

09:39   LINDA: They don't talk; they don't talk. (*Linda is again making a categorical statement, implying that they don't talk at all.*)

09:41   VIRGINIA (in a challenging tone):   For how many years have they not talked? (*Virginia challenges Linda's overgeneralization, making it more extreme by asking, "How many years?"*)

09:43   LINDA: Well, my father's passed away now, so they're *really* not talking, but—(laughter) For—forever, forty years. (*Linda has reiterated an extreme generalization that can't be true. Before Linda can forgive her mother, she needs to be able to see her in a more balanced way. Virginia will interrupt her and then challenge Linda's perception of her mother—still in a friendly, joking way.*)

09:53   VIRGINIA: Now, wait a minute, now just a minute here. [repetition] How do you suppose they got—(Virginia turns to Linda's "mother" and Randy, who is now playing the role of her father.) Would you please embrace each other? I would like you (Linda) to see them embracing each other. You (parents) are now sixteen and fourteen. Embrace please. (Linda's "parents" embrace, and Linda laughs loudly.) Is that when they met, when they were very young? How old were they? (*Linda has been focused on her mother's behavior toward her during her own lifetime. Now Virginia is focusing Linda's attention on her parents' behavior before Linda was born. Virginia presupposes some kind of positive loving relationship to enrich Linda's picture of her parents.*)

10:04   LINDA: No, they were older. Thirty, mid-thirties.

10:07   VIRGINIA: All right, so they are mid-thirties, but you know that happened?

10:11   LINDA: That they embraced?

10:12   VIRGINIA: Yes.

10:13   LINDA: I doubt it. (Linda and the group laugh. *Again Linda makes an extreme statement, denying that her parents had any positive feelings for each other. Virginia will challenge this in order to make Linda's perceptions of her mother more realistic and balanced.*)

10:14   VIRGINIA: Well, now wait a minute. Wait a minute. [repetition] Did he—did her mother work with a marriage broker or—? How was this? (*By playfully asking if her parents got together by using a marriage broker, Virginia is exaggerating Linda's impli-*

cation that her parents had no positive feelings for each other in a way that is intended to prod Linda into correcting this.)

10:23   LINDA: I think they met on a blind date. (*Again Linda implicitly continues to deny any positive reason for her parents to come together.*)

10:26   VIRGINIA: Well, you can—a lot of people meet on a blind date and you just meet and go right on by. *These two didn't do that. (Again Virginia is asking Linda to recognize some positive feelings between her parents.*)

10:31   LINDA: I know.

10:32   VIRGINIA: How come?

10:34   LINDA: Because she was lonely and he wanted somebody to save her.

10:39   VIRGINIA: Save *her*?

10:40   LINDA: Umhm.

10:41   VIRGINIA: Or *him*?

10:42   LINDA: Ah, save *him*.

10:43   VIRGINIA (lightly):   Well, that sounds like "par for the course." OK. (Linda laughs.) Umhm. (looking down left) All right, now, do you suppose that they might have met anybody else that he would think she was lonely, but he could also have found some other people that were lonely, and she could have found somebody that she wanted to keep her company. Do you suppose that ever happened? That they found some other people? (skeptically) Was this the only catch that they could make? (*Virginia continues to ask for information about Linda's parents' attraction to each other, to broaden and enrich Linda's perceptions and to change her distorted generalization about her parents.*)

11:12   LINDA (thoughtfully):   That's a tough question . . . . I think that the timing was right, that they were both getting older, and they felt that they had better do something quick because it was going to get too late. (*Linda continues to deny implicitly that her parents had any positive reasons for marrying. Virginia again challenges this directly.*)

11:23   VIRGINIA (skeptically):   Now, do you *really* believe that?

11:24   LINDA: (smiling broadly):   No, I don't! (laughter)

11:25   VIRGINIA: All right. I don't either. I don't either. (*Virginia emphasizes that she is agreeing with Linda. The phrase "I don't either" implies it is Linda's idea and Virginia is agreeing with it. This makes it easier for Linda to experience it as her own perception, not something that Virginia induced her to think by repeated questioning. [9:53 – 11:23]*) But that's the "PR" that goes out. (*By using the term "PR"—public relations—Virginia makes the distinction between perception and reality* [model of the world].) Yes, because you didn't *see* what was going on then. (*Virginia shifts Linda's old perceptions into the past with "didn't" and "then," and uses the embedded instruction to "see what was going on" in the present. Next she goes on to paint a picture that will be more useful for Linda, shifting to a lower, more serious tone of voice.*) What I *can* believe is that they were both shy, and I can see him as being in a family where he had to get all the other kids educated or something before—or his father dying—I don't know what. But they had to put off marriage for some reason. And so their "gonad-flapping" wouldn't have been quite as obvious, but it had to be there."

(*Virginia shifts Linda's focus from her parents' behavior to their inner feelings and motives by suggesting that perhaps they were shy, or had to carry out other responsibilities before considering marriage. She also presupposes that they were sexually attracted to each other by using an unusual and humorous term: "gonad-flapping." It doesn't matter whether Virginia is correct in any of these guesses, as long as she directs Linda's attention to what her parents' internal experience of attraction might have been in their early life together— again broadening Linda's perceptions of her parents.*)

11:52   LINDA: Umhm.

11:53   VIRGINIA: How many times did they do it? How many kids did they have? (*The indirect reference to sex again asks Linda to think about her parents' attraction to each other.*)

11:56   LINDA: Three.

11:57   VIRGINIA (lightly, as if considering the score in a game): Three. Well, that's pretty good. (laughter) All right. So these two people, when you *saw* them, you didn't *see this*. (*Saying "when you saw them you didn't see this" puts Linda's old perceptions into the past, immediately followed by what she is now seeing about her parent's earlier life together. "Saw . . . see this" is an embedded command that tells Linda, "Whenever you think of those old perceptions, you will see this"—the more positive feelings that brought her parents together* [temporal predicate shift]. *"You didn't see" presupposes that it was there. Then Virginia goes on to suggest other new perceptions for Linda to add to her old and incomplete images of her parents.*)

12:05 VIRGINIA: You didn't see what brought them together. (*Again Virginia uses the same linguistic form. The negation, "You didn't," introduces an embedded command: "See what brought them together."*) Because my hunch is that they were both "scared chickens." (Virginia turns to Linda's "mother.") All right, would you put your arms like that. (Virginia demonstrates by crossing her arms across her chest, and "mother" follows.) Yeah, scared to death. "I don't want to feel; I don't want to—I'm afraid of this happening or that happening." What do you know about her (gesturing toward Linda's "mother") life growing up? (*Asking about her mother's childhood directs Linda's attention to additional information that will broaden and deepen Linda's understanding of her mother.*)

12:23 LINDA: *Very* difficult.

12:24 VIRGINIA: What was difficult about it? (*Linda's complaint is that her mother made life difficult for her. Now she says that her mother's childhood was also difficult. This similarity provides an opportunity for Linda to understand her mother rather than to fight her.* Virginia steps in between Linda and her "mother," facing Linda.) Now you talk to me. (*Virginia asks Linda to talk to her, not her "mother," because she wants the information about her mother's difficulties to stay separate from Linda's own difficulties for the time being. It will also be easier for Linda to talk to Virginia than to her "mother" about this. At this point, Virginia wants information. She will go for the direct encounter and emotional response later, after she has information about Linda's mother's difficulties.*)

12:28 LINDA: Umm, a father that was domineering, and perhaps abusive and ah—

12:33   VIRGINIA: So she had been used to being slapped around.

12:36   LINDA: Right. Italian immigrants, so there was lots of, "You need to behave a certain way so that people don't perceive you as being different or weird," and lots of, ah—she wasn't allowed to be with boys or date men, so that was often very difficult. If he even saw her in the same block with a man, she was punished, and those kinds of things. (Linda's hand gestures as she speaks are eloquent but hard to capture in words.)

12:53   VIRGINIA: Did he beat her up?

12:55   LINDA: Um, it's hard to say, but probably.

12:58   VIRGINIA: All right, OK.

12:59   LINDA: We don't have that kind of communication, so I don't know for sure.

13:01   VIRGINIA: All right. Now what are you *feeling*, what are you *feeling* [repetition] about what you are just saying, about the kind of experiences that this lady had before she ever thought of being your mother—before she even thought of being married? (*Virginia has just gathered information about the mother's childhood, separate from her experiences as a mother to Linda. Since it's likely that Linda has more useful feelings in response to this, Virginia asks about them.*)

13:13   LINDA (softly):   I have been feeling a lot of empathy for her. (*This can be thought of as context reframing, since Linda now expresses more positive feelings for the same person in a different context, earlier in time. Eliciting these feelings is a step toward incorporating these new feelings into Linda's present interactions with her mother.*)

13:16   VIRGINIA: OK. Now, I wonder if you can translate that even further into appreciation. [embedded question] (*Virginia knows that empathy is not enough, so she immediately works to develop these feelings. By using the word "translate," Virginia presupposes that empathy and appreciation have equivalent meanings, rather than distinctly different ones.*) Let me tell you what I have in mind. (softly) She's still trying. (*Now Virginia turns Linda's attention to her mother's good intentions [meaning reframing] using a soft voice tone. By delet-*

ing what her mother is trying to do, Virginia invites Linda to fill in her own positive motives—trying to express love, be a good mother, etc.)

13:25 LINDA: Umhm.

13:26 VIRGINIA (softly): But what does she say to you? She says in effect to you, "You need to be fat, because if you're fat, you'll probably be healthy." *(By directing Linda's attention to her mother's good intention—wanting Linda to be healthy—she reframes the meaning of one of Linda's complaints: her mother saying, "You're too skinny.")* That's one of the things that people thought in those days. *(By focusing Linda's attention on her mother's past environment, Virginia establishes a new cause-effect: the mother's concern with weight is a result of antiquated thinking.)*

13:39 VIRGINIA: What was one of the other things you gave me?

13:41 LINDA: I'm too loud.

13:43 VIRGINIA: Oh, "You talk too loud." All right. (softly) Now, I have a feeling that loudness of voice is associated in her mind with trouble. *(This reframes the meaning of Linda's mother's criticism—"You're too loud"—as a fearful response to being beaten and abused in her childhood. It's not actually a response to Linda's behavior at all.)*

13:53 VIRGINIA: Now I also know something else. It was easier for you to connect with your father than it was with her. *(The first sentence refers to, and presupposes, the second sentence, which is ambiguous. It can have either (or both) of two meanings: "It was easier for Linda to connect with her father than it was for Linda to connect with her mother," or "It was easier for Linda to connect with her father than it was for her mother to connect with her husband." The latter meaning provides an implicit parallel between Linda and her mother. Her mother also had difficulty connecting with people.)*

13:58 VIRGINIA: So she (gesturing toward "mother") looks at you and she feels all the lost parts. *("The lost parts" is unspecified. Because of the prior ambiguity it can mean mother's inability to connect with Linda, or to connect with her husband, or both.)* That isn't your fault or her fault. [no blame] But this woman (stepping aside and gesturing toward Linda's "mother") really never ever felt that she got anything out of life. (*Again Virginia directs Linda's attention to her mother's feelings instead of her behavior*.) OK? All that does is help her to understand this—for *you* to understand this.

(*Linda began by focusing on the cause-effect: "Mother's behavior causes my bad feelings." By backing up in time to her mother's childhood, Virginia establishes a new cause-effect: "Mother's abusive childhood caused her bad feelings and critical behavior." This redefines her mother's critical behavior. It's part of her mother's response to an unpleasant childhood; it's not really about Linda at all.*)

14:15   VIRGINIA: It doesn't mean anything about loving her. It doesn't mean that this is a pleasant thing. It doesn't mean that it is *wonderful* to hear somebody say you are too skinny.

(*Virginia is saying here that thinking about her mother's internal experiences and feelings helps Linda to understand her behavior and appreciate her as a person, separate from liking what she does. By starting with a negation—"It doesn't mean . . . "—Virginia summarizes and paces Linda's understanding in a way that also creates opportunities for giving positive embedded commands: "loving her," "This is a pleasant thing," and "It is wonderful to hear somebody say you are too skinny." Notice how different it would be if Virginia had said something like, "This means that you still hate her behavior, and it's very unpleasant for you, and it's horrible for you to hear somebody say you're too skinny." This would also pace Linda's experience, but without providing positive alternatives, it would only amplify her unhappiness. The linguistic form that Virginia uses here is the same one she used earlier [11:57, 12:05]. She starts with a negation, "It doesn't mean . . . " followed by what she would like Linda to experience, in the form of an embedded command. This is a variation of the negative command. Statements like "Don't think of pink elephants" or "Don't feel good now" typically result in the listener—even the reader—thinking of pink elephants or feeling good. Some people might object that Virginia wouldn't want Linda to think being criticized was a pleasant thing; however this is exactly the meaning that Linda arrives at much later in the session [49:31].*)

14:23   VIRGINIA: By the way, I got—is she (gesturing toward "mother") still around?

14:24   LINDA: Umhm.

14:25   VIRGINIA: Next time she says that, you can bet—because you've already developed a system where she's going to say that, and then you are going to have to do whatever you do. Now, the next time she says that— (Virginia turns to Linda's "mother") Would you please tell her that she's too skinny? (*Since Virginia has reframed the mother's behavior in general as meaning "she had a tough life" rather than meaning something bad about Linda, Linda is able to feel new feelings toward her mother. Virginia's next task is to connect these new feelings to the mother's specific behaviors that used to make Linda feel bad.*)

(*Virginia begins to describe the cybernetic loop of stimulus-response between Linda and her mother. She then shifts to enacting it, which will give Linda a more intense personal understanding* [association]. *This will also give Virginia an opportunity to intervene and change Linda's response if it's not yet resourceful, or if it's in a form that would not be likely to get a useful response from her mother.*)

14:34   "MOTHER":   You're too skinny.

14:36   VIRGINIA: Now (Linda) would you go up to her (gesturing toward her "mother") and *thank her for noticing you* [linkage and direct command]. (*Many people would quickly accept this meaning reframe and command, even though it's a jump from the foregoing discussion about understanding her mother's behavior as a result of her difficult childhood. When Linda hesitates, Virginia pushes her toward her "mother." Linda looks to the side and appears reluctant, but does go over to her "mother" and takes her hands. The group laughs. Up to this point Linda has quickly and willingly done everything Virginia asked her to do. However, Linda balks at Virginia's attempt to reframe her mother's comments as evidence that she notices her; Virginia persists.*)

14:40   VIRGINIA: Take her hand and thank her for noticing you [direct command], and then say, "You know, I've been meaning to share [this] with you before. I know you've often noticed me like this, but I would just like to tell you how I feel about my body." But *first you thank her for noticing you* [direct command], and then say you'd like to share how you feel about your body, because I think she thinks you're going to die if you don't eat enough.

(Virginia repeats the reframe that her mother's concern about Linda's weight is evidence of her caring, but Linda gives no evidence of accepting the reframe or of being willing to follow Virginia's instruction to thank her mother for noticing her. Since Linda is not responding fully, Virginia next turns to the group and shifts the focus from Linda specifically to the more general case.)

14:59   VIRGINIA: Do you know how that used to be within the circles? It's not very long ago, you know, that "I show my love by food." And if you stay skinny, it means you don't get it. *(Virginia steps into the role of Linda's mother by saying, "I show my love by food." Since Linda has positive feelings for Virginia, this makes it easier for Linda to consider and take on this new understanding.)*

15:09   LINDA: Well, my mother's Italian. That will give you some insight.

15:12   VIRGINIA: Yeah, I know that, but you don't have to be Italian to do that. (She turns to the group.) How many of you had mothers who—where you got love, you were supposed to get love through the food? Let's see. Yeah, sure. *(Virginia uses the group's response to make Linda's mother's concern about her weight more ordinary* [normalization].*) Do you do that? (Virginia asks Linda if she also does what her mother does, searching for another similarity between them.)*

15:23   LINDA (apparently confused):   What? Yes. *(It is not clear whether Linda realizes what she is saying yes to.)*

15:26   VIRGINIA: OK. Well, all right, maybe you can stop now. *("You can stop now" clearly refers to the food topic. Yet it also has a broader meaning: "You can stop old behavior and have new choices.")* OK, and you will show your love with your arms and not with your food, because that was never made for that. (softly) But *she* thought so. Now, as you thank her for that, what do you feel? *(In her continuing effort to get Linda to thank her mother, Virginia first presupposes that she is already doing it by saying, "As you thank her . . ." Then she focuses her attention with "What do you feel?" and follows with a direct command.)* Thank her for noticing you. You're not thanking her for telling you what she's telling you, but for *noticing* you. *(Virginia again separates the mother's positive intention from her unpleasant behavior. Linda closes her eyes and takes a breath, but keeps her mouth tightly closed.*) Are you aware of that? (*By saying "Are you aware of that," everything Virginia just said becomes presupposed.*) What does that feel like?

15:46   LINDA: I'm having trouble doing it.

15:48   VIRGINIA: I know, because for so long—(Linda laughs.) Let me tell you what she looked like to you. (*When Virginia says "what she looked like to you," she is pacing Linda's perceptions. At the same time, she uses the past tense "looked" and introduces the presupposition that this was Linda's perception by saying "to you," and that her mother was actually different from what she "looked like" [model of the world].*) Would you put your fingers up here? (*Virginia demonstrates by pointing one finger up from each temple, like devil's horns, exaggerating Linda's perceptions in such a way that she will almost have to re-evaluate them. Linda and her "mother" both put their fingers to their temples in the same way. Linda smiles and the group laughs.*) That's right. (Linda puts her fingers down again, while her "mother" keeps her fingers at her temples.) And that she was trying to make your life miserable. Right? (*Since Linda didn't respond to Virginia's attempts to ascribe positive purposes to her mother's behavior, Virginia reverses her approach and exaggerates the opposite possibility—that her mother was evil and her intentions were bad. This regains rapport with Linda. Even as Virginia does this, she is loosening Linda's beliefs about her mother in subtle ways by using past tense [model of the world], and by exaggerating her statement of "evil" so much that it begins to seem ridiculous.*)

15:59   LINDA (strongly):   Absolutely!

16:00   VIRGINIA: OK. Now everything you saw sort of added up to that, and with where you were, that could be your awareness of that. (*Again Virginia uses past tense—"saw," "added up," "were"— to describe Linda's perceptions and awareness.* [model of the world]) But she's really not a miserable lady. [temporal predicate shift] (Linda's "mother" continues to hold her fingers at her temples. Linda laughs.) She just *looks* like one. (The group laughs.) Right? (*Virginia continues to make the distinction between Linda's perceptions of her mother, in the past, and what she really is, in the present, in a way that emphasizes and paces Linda's perceptions* [model of the world].)

16:14   LINDA (laughing):   Yes!

16:15   VIRGINIA: All right, now, what are you feeling right now as you are looking at her?

16:18   LINDA (laughing):   She looks ridiculous! (*The group laughs. Previously Linda was very serious about her mother being a "devil." Now she is laughing at the idea—even though she still believes it.*)

16:20   VIRGINIA (to Linda's "mother"):   All right, so put your fingers down at this moment. (To Linda, touching her elbow)   What I'm asking you to do at this time—(Virginia looks down and left, recalling what Linda said earlier.) See, when you came up here you said you feel power, and then you feel this wimpy business. Didn't you tell me that?

16:31   LINDA: Umhm.

16:32   VIRGINIA (joking):   I've got the right person and all that, OK. When you feel what you call "wimpy"— Would you ("mother") give her . . . point the finger, (Virginia and Linda's "mother" both point their fingers at Linda) say, "You're too skinny and you talk too loud, and you don't take care of your music. You're blessed and talented, and I sit around and I see all that, and you don't do a thing with it. You're doing it to spite me. You know I want a concert pianist, or I don't know what it is, it doesn't matter, because the same message will get through." So tell her all that. (*This puts Linda into an associated experience of the difficult interaction with her mother, and allows Virginia to find out exactly what Linda's response is at this moment, providing clues about possible useful next steps.*)

16:57   LINDA'S "MOTHER" (still pointing her finger at Linda): You're too skinny, and you're just sitting around not doing anything with all that talent, and that really is a reflection on me. And I just want you to be more powerful, and keep your voice down and—

17:13   LINDA: Spffft. ("Bronx cheer")

17:14   VIRGINIA: OK, so what did you do when you did that? How did you take what she was giving you? (*By asking, "How did you take . . . " Virginia presupposes that Linda has a choice of alterna-*

tives. By using the word "giving," Virginia presupposes that Linda's mother's behavior is a gift—in contrast to describing it as a "lecture" or "attack," for instance. She turns to Linda's "mother.") You can put that (pointing finger) down now.

17:27   LINDA: I felt this burning sensation in my—in this center area (gesturing just below her ribs) and I—then I could just hear—it's the same "tape" (gesturing with both hands moving toward her, like waves washing over her), and so I just started—I felt myself closing down a little bit more (gesturing with both hands closing together in front of her face), and then feeling that anger, that—where I hadn't—I'm confused with what you're saying. When do I say to her, "I don't want to hear that anymore," (shaking her head "No") and when do I say, (taking a step toward "mother") "Gee, thanks, Mom, for telling me and noticing. How wonderful it is for you to notice that." When—?

17:48   VIRGINIA: Yes, that's the first step. That's the first step. (Virginia silently looks at Linda with arched eyebrows, nodding slightly. Linda looks back without speaking for five seconds and then smiles. *Virginia knows what is useful for Linda to do to move toward forgiveness, and directly confronts her with the need to appreciate first in order to reach forgiveness and resolution.*)

17:56   LINDA: Is telling her where to get off? (*Linda's response shows that her earlier refusal to say "thank you for noticing me" stems from believing that she needs to confront her mother in order to resolve her resentment—a common misunderstanding. Even though Virginia has repeatedly made a distinction between intention and behavior, Linda still needs to experience that she can thank her mother for her good intention, even though she still dislikes the critical behavior.*)

17:58   VIRGINIA (curtly):   No. (*Virginia knows confrontation would only create more difficulties.*)

17:59   LINDA: Oh.

18:00   VIRGINIA: That's not the first step. Thanking her for noticing you [is].

18:03   LINDA: Oh, thanking.

18:15   VIRGINIA: That's the first step. Now what do you have to do to thank her for her—for that—taking that first step—thanking her for *noticing* you? (*Notice how often Virginia has repeated the phrase "thanking her for noticing you." By asking, "What do you have to do to thank her . . . " Virginia requests information about what will have to happen first for her to do it, presupposing that Linda will eventually do it.*)

18:17   LINDA: It seems I have to . . . shift my perceptions from (*Linda gestures with both hands in a horizontal circle, back and forth—an exquisite gesture that indicates her ability to take her mother's perceptual position*) seeing that as a criticism and a way of putting me down (making a jabbing motion with her right index finger) and seeing that as her way of loving me. (*Linda gestures from her "mother" to her own chest, the same eloquent gesture of connection that she used previously with Virginia as she described loving connection [3:25]. Both verbally and nonverbally, Linda is providing Virginia with a specific way to reframe her mother's criticism by seeing it as "her way of loving" Linda.*)

18:32   VIRGINIA: Well, it might not be that, but I think it is some of that. Now, do you have any kids?

18:36   LINDA: No. (*Linda has been judging her mother harshly—for judging her! By asking about kids—and a moment later about "anybody close to you"—Virginia is searching for someone with whom to help Linda discover her own judging in a context of closeness and warm feelings—an example that will show she can judge someone she loves dearly.*)

18:37   VIRGINIA: Do you have anybody close to you?

18:38   LINDA (softly):   I have a wonderful husband.

18:39   VIRGINIA: All right, would you pick him out here? (Virginia gestures toward the group.) I want to see what you do with him. Any husband will do. (Linda laughs and the group laughs.)

18:47   LINDA (scanning the group and then gesturing to a man): Any husband will do.

18:49   VIRGINIA: Yeah, well, sure. OK. Now, tell me how you judge him. (Linda's "husband" comes up and stands in front of Linda.)

18:55 LINDA: He's—how do I judge him?

18:56 VIRGINIA: Yes, yes, what—

18:57 LINDA: He's wonderful and kind and sensitive.

18:59 VIRGINIA: Isn't there anything wrong with him?

19:01 LINDA (softly): Yeah.

19:02 VIRGINIA: All right, tell me what's wrong with him.

19:03 LINDA (softly): Well, he's a little wimpy sometimes.

19:05 VIRGINIA: All right, OK. (Linda and the group laugh.) So, "You're just a wimp." (Virginia points her finger at Linda's "husband.") Let's do that one. (Virginia reaches down for Linda's right hand and brings it up in a straight-armed pointing gesture.) Well, I'm going to exaggerate it. "You're just a wimp—" (*Virginia asks Linda to experience her own judging behavior fully by acting it out in the present* [association]. *By calling this an exaggeration, Virginia has a better chance of getting Linda to do it without feeling the need to qualify or excuse it.*)

19:10 LINDA: But I don't do this to him. (*Linda is reluctant.*)

19:11 VIRGINIA: I know.

19:11 LINDA: OK.

19:12 VIRGINIA: You *think* it, though.

19:13 LINDA: Well, no, we talk about it. (*Linda is still reluctant, then shifts to willingness.*) OK. You're just a wimp. (resentfully) Why don't you—why don't *you* assert yourself once in a while, instead of having *me* have to be the one that says "No" to people? (Virginia nods approvingly.)

(*Linda has just congruently criticized her husband, whom she previously described as someone she loves—"wonderful and kind and sensitive." This example shows that she can criticize someone she loves deeply. This is a counterexample to Linda's belief that her mother's criticism of her is proof that she doesn't love her. Next Virginia will presuppose a parallel between Linda's judging and her mother's judging. If Linda can judge someone she loves, so can her mother.*)

19:22 VIRGINIA: All right. Close your eyes now, and just let yourself (*Saying "Close your eyes now, and . . . " links an easy task with what follows* [linkage]. *"Let yourself . . . " presupposes that whatever she describes next will happen automatically unless Linda interferes.* Virginia places her hand gently on the small of Linda's back.) into how you feel about that wonderful judge inside yourself (*By saying "wonderful" in a warm, congruent voice, Virginia makes it easier for Linda to accept and recognize her own judging. Virginia directs Linda's attention to her feeling response to being a judge.* Linda smiles, then laughs shortly.) which your mother also has. (*By saying "which your mother also has," Virginia gently presupposes an identity between Linda and her mother.*)

19:30 LINDA: I don't like it.

19:31 VIRGINIA: Now I want you to keep your eyes closed and look at that judge [linkage]. (*Now Virginia asks Linda to see the judging behavior she has just expressed as separate from her* [dissociation].)

19:35 VIRGINIA: That judge is a possibility for you to take a look—the kind of judge *you've* got and the kind of judge your mother had was pretty hard on both of you. (*Virginia restates the identity between Linda and her mother, and goes on to include the mother as a victim of this judging, rather than a judge. The presupposed message is, "Your mother also has a judge who is hard on her." The judge is no longer the mother, but is redescribed as separate from the mother, who also feels the unpleasantness of being judged. Linda nods.*) Do you notice that? (*Presupposing all the foregoing*)

19:45 LINDA: Umhm.

19:46 VIRGINIA: OK. Now, judges can let people go free; they can imprison them. They can *also* take what they see in front of them (Virginia gestures palm up in front of Linda's face) and give guidance. Now, what kind of a judge do you want for you? (*Virginia is apparently offering Linda a choice among three alternatives. Actually she is restricting Linda's choices to these three, since it's unlikely that Linda will take the time to think up a fourth possibility. And since the first two choices—freedom and imprisonment—are predictably unacceptable to Linda, it's really no choice at all, but a way of gracefully offering Linda a new behavior that is balanced between judging and indifference. This is also emphasized by Virginia's hand gesture right in front of Linda's face.)*

19:58   LINDA: A guiding judge.

20:00   VIRGINIA: All right. Now open your eyes now, and think, "I now have a guiding judge inside of me." OK? (*"Now open your eyes now" is a request that Linda knows is easy to do. "And" is a hypnotic link to what Virginia wants her to do next, implying that it will also be easy. Asking Linda to "think" she has a guiding judge is a first step toward presupposing that she has one. Since you can think anything, Linda won't object to trying it out. Next Virginia will shift from asking Linda to "think" she has a guiding judge to presupposing it.)*

20:05   LINDA: Umhm.

20:07   VIRGINIA: Now, when you have that guiding judge (*"When" presupposes that Linda has a guiding judge*) how can you use (*"How can you use" presupposes that Linda will do it; it's only a question of how*) that guiding judge to be able to signal to your husband—like later you will signal to your mother— (*This presupposes that Linda will later do the same with her mother. This is another clear indication that Virginia has a definite plan for what she will do with Linda later in this session.)* "I hear you. I hear you, and let me share with you what happens for *me* when that happens." That's your guiding judge. Just let the words come out of this beautiful throat of yours and see what happens. (*"Let the words come out" presupposes they will come out on their own; all Linda has to do is allow it. She uses a presupposed compliment—"this beautiful throat of yours"— to help access a positive, loving state from which to "judge.")*

(*A summary of what Virginia says in this paragraph is: "If you think you have a guiding judge, you will have a guiding judge, and therefore you will say more useful things to your husband, and later to your mother, and all this will happen without any conscious effort." This kind of hypnotic communication may not be "logical," but it's compelling when it's presupposed and delivered congruently.)*

20:34   LINDA (pausing for six seconds and then smiling slightly, with a soft voice):   I— (moving both feet a couple of inches closer to her "husband") It would be helpful to me . . . (Linda gestures toward her "husband" with her left hand palm up—*indicating more feeling involvement than with the previous pointing and judging*) if sometimes . . . you would assert yourself and be the person that says "No" to people on the telephone, because it's real difficult (Linda places her left hand on her chest) for me to be in that role all the time.

(Linda's communication with her "husband" is straightforward and direct—in contrast to her previous resentful blaming [19:18]. *Since Virginia has presupposed that Linda will later do the same with her mother* [20:17], *this is, in effect, a rehearsal for later speaking directly with her mother.)*

20:47 VIRGINIA (softly): OK, now close your eyes, and I want to ask you to ask yourself, "Is it possible that you have ever . . . done the same? [linkage and switch referential index] *(By gracefully asking, "Is it possible"* [conversational postulate] *Virginia also makes it easier for Linda to answer "yes" to the question than if she had asked, "Have you done the same?" or, "Are you as bad as he is?")*

20:58 LINDA: Been a wimp, you mean?

21:00 VIRGINIA: Yeah.

21:01 LINDA: Of course.

21:02 VIRGINIA: In your language.

21:03 LINDA: Umhm.

21:04 VIRGINIA (softly): All right, now look up with your beautiful eyes and just look at him and say, "I know what wimping is, I'm working on it, too." [linkage] *(By using the embedded compliment "your beautiful eyes," Virginia brings a feeling of love and acceptance to what might otherwise seem like admitting a flaw. Linda and the group laugh heartily.)*

21:11 LINDA: Umhm. *(Although Linda has not overtly done what Virginia asked, her response clearly indicates that she has done it willingly in her internal experience, so it's not necessary to ask her to do it out loud. By having Linda acknowledge this same flaw in herself, she helps Linda create a relationship of equality between herself and her husband, rather than a relationship of judge to a person being judged. As Linda internalizes this equality it will change her behavior, and that will make others more receptive to what Linda has to say. By acknowledging this similarity between herself and her husband, Linda is also implicitly acknowledging her similarity with her mother, since Virginia has previously equated Linda's husband with her mother [20:17].)*

21:13 VIRGINIA: All right. Now when you discovered (Virginia faces Linda and takes both her hands in hers) your own wimpy—which you said, you nodded—

21:18 LINDA: Umhm. Right.

21:19 VIRGINIA: All right, one of the things that bothered you about that—when your husband did it—was that it put you in a space where you didn't want to be.

21:31 LINDA: All the time.

21:32 VIRGINIA: Well, that's the way you accepted it.

21:34 LINDA: OK.

21:35 VIRGINIA: OK. There's no reason you have to accept it, but you did. (*Here Virginia helps Linda shift her focus to her own part in the interaction. Rather than experiencing herself as "helpless" in response to her husband's behavior, she can choose to accept it or not. This places Linda in an active rather than passive role.*)

21:38 LINDA: OK.

21:39 VIRGINIA (stepping aside so that Linda can face her "mother" again, Virginia continues to hold Linda's left hand with her own right hand, and speaks to Linda's "mother"): All right. Now stand outside just a little bit here, now. And [Linda] remember when I said, "Can you thank her (gesturing toward Linda's "mother") for noticing you"? [15:26]

21:48 LINDA: Umhm.

21:49 VIRGINIA: And you said, "I don't want to do it." [15:46] Now, what did it *mean* to you to thank her (gesturing toward Linda's "mother") for noticing you? (*Virginia starts by describing this incident in the past: "remember when I said," "you said," "what did it mean . . . ." She could have used present tense: "What does it mean . . . ." Putting Linda's objection in the past tense is a gentle suggestion to dissociate from it, making it easier for Linda to think about the meaning "back there." It is also an invitation to leave the objection in the past and move on to a new meaning that would be congruent with her thanking her mother. Linda follows Virginia's lead and describes the event in past tense.*)

22:00   LINDA: I think it meant that um . . . if I acknowledged that . . . she—Let's see, that I was almost going to have to defend myself *more*, maybe. If I acknowledged that she noticed that I was thin, that it would open up a whole new—

22:19   VIRGINIA (strongly):   *No, that's not what I said!*

22:21   LINDA: Oh.

22:22   VIRGINIA: There's a very different thing from *noticing me.* (*Since "noticing me" is emphatically marked out as an embedded command it also has the meaning of telling Linda to pay attention and notice what Virginia is telling her to do.*)

22:24   LINDA: OK, tell me what you're saying here. (*At this point Virginia has used essentially the same sentence ten times* [14:38, 14:40, 14:50, 15:33, 15:36, 15:40, 18:00, 18:05, 21:39, 22:49], *but Linda still hasn't understood it, so Virginia persists.*)

22:27   VIRGINIA: I'm saying, "Thank you for noticing *me.*" (*"Noticing me" is different from "noticing I am thin."*)

22:31   LINDA: Umhm! (Linda looks up with sudden recognition and laughs.)

22:33   VIRGINIA: Isn't it better to be noticed, no matter what for?

22:38   LINDA: Boy! (smiling and shaking her head slowly from side to side, still uncertain)

22:40   VIRGINIA: Let's just see what happens to you. (to her "mother") Would you move back a little bit. (to Linda) And just say— let your body say, (*Again, Virginia uses "let" and adds "your body say," presupposing that Linda's body—not her mind—will speak if she will only allow it to happen.*) "Thank you for noticing *me.*" [direct command] Let's see what happens. (*By framing this at both the beginning and end of the instruction with "Let's see what happens," Virginia focuses Linda's attention on what will occur during and after she does what Virginia asked. This presupposes she will do it, and tends to take Linda's attention away from thinking about whether she wants to do it or not.*)

22:49   LINDA (reluctantly):   Thank you for noticing me.

22:51   VIRGINIA: All right. That's all you're saying "thank you" for.

22:54   LINDA: Umhm.

22:55   VIRGINIA: All right. How did that feel inside?

22:57   LINDA: Dishonest.

22:58   VIRGINIA: Ah hah. What's dishonest about it?

23:01   LINDA (gesturing toward her "mother" with her right hand, palm up) Because I'm *tired* of only being noticed by her in negative ways.

23:05   VIRGINIA (impatiently):   You want to be noticed differently, and I'm giving you a way to *do it.* [embedded command] (*Virginia paces Linda's wanting a more positive response from her mother and links this motivation to what Virginia is asking her to do.*)

23:07   LINDA: Or *not*—I'm willing to even *not* be noticed.

23:09   VIRGINIA: I *know*, and that would be a *terrible* thing. (*Virginia knows that the isolation of not being noticed at all would be far more harmful than the conflict involved in being noticed in negative ways—a fact that small children who are ignored display implicitly in their continued striving for contact, no matter how painful. Linda laughs.*)

23:13   VIRGINIA: Tell me what's going on in your objection business here. (*Since Linda has an objection to doing what Virginia asks, Virginia needs to know what the objection is, and satisfy it, before Linda can proceed congruently.*)

23:17   LINDA: Because I think that my mother only notices me in negative ways. (*Linda continues to focus on her mother's behavior and her own feelings in response to that behavior, rather than on her mother's positive intention in noticing.*)

23:21   VIRGINIA: OK, would you like to *change that*? (*Virginia uses Linda's objection to build motivation, giving the embedded command "change that."*)

23:23   LINDA (emphatically):   Yes!

23:24   VIRGINIA: All right. Now—

23:25   LINDA: I think. (Linda smiles, recognizing her ambivalence.)

23:26   VIRGINIA: "You think?" (Linda laughs and nods, and she and Virginia both smile; the group laughs. Virginia looks down and to the left.) All right, I want to now make a big concept out of this, and let's see what happens.

23:31   LINDA: OK.

23:33   VIRGINIA: Your mother really never believed that you cared about her. (*Virginia is again asking Linda to consider her mother's thoughts and feelings, so that Linda can begin to understand her mother's behavior in a different way. More specifically, she is taking Linda's implicit complaint—"My mother didn't care about me"—and reversing it to "You didn't care about your mother." However, Virginia softens this by stating it only as the mother's belief* [model of the world], *not as fact.*)

23:37   LINDA: Umhm.

23:38   VIRGINIA: I'm sure. I'm sure she thought you cared much more for your father. [model of the world] (*This is something that Virginia already knows Linda agrees with fully, but restating it adds strength to this new attempt to get Linda to consider her mother's feelings and motivations—which will give new meaning to the mother's critical behavior.*)

23:40   LINDA: Umhm.

23:41   VIRGINIA: Can you visualize (looking up), or even understand in some way, how a woman could feel that one of her children (Virginia gestures toward Linda) didn't care about her? (Virginia gestures toward "mother." *By using "visualize," Virginia begins by asking Linda to think of this dissociated, using a conversational postulate, and then broadens the possibilities to the general, "or even understand in some way," which can serve as a bridge toward association and identification with her mother. Saying "a woman" instead of "your mother" makes it easier for Linda to think of the situation in a general way, or even to identify with her mother—Linda is also, after all, a woman. Linda has been presupposing that her mother doesn't care about her, so Virginia knows that Linda knows what it feels like to have someone not care about her. Linda has also been vigorously claiming that she and her mother are very different. Asking in this general way gently asks Linda to begin to see that she and her mother are similar, rather than different.)*

23:47　LINDA:　Umhm. (*Although Linda agrees, she is not responding as fully as she could, so Virginia continues to try to get Linda to experience more fully what her mother must have felt.*)

23:48　VIRGINIA:　All right. Have you ever had the feeling that somebody didn't care about you? They cared more about somebody else? (*Virginia could have said directly, "Look, you feel that your mother didn't care about you." Instead she uses a general question—"Have you ever had the feeling that somebody didn't care about you?" This allows Linda to find any example of this, without Virginia directly confronting her with the similarity between herself and her mother. At the same time, it is an explicit instruction to Linda to put herself "in her mother's place"* [switch referential index] *in regard to this feeling.*)

23:53　LINDA:　Oh, *definitely!* (*Now Linda is responding fully.*)

23:54　VIRGINIA:　All right. So you know what that feeling is like.

23:56　LINDA:　Umhm.

23:57　VIRGINIA:　Now, your mother (gesturing toward "mother"), I think, has the same feeling. Now let's see what happens. Your mother has to be on the protection side for herself with you. Can you *see how that would be?* [conversational postulate and embedded command] (*Linda has previously expressed the need to protect herself from her mother's not caring. By saying that the mother had to protect herself, Virginia draws another implicit parallel between Linda and her mother.*)

24:09　LINDA:　Umhm.

24:10   VIRGINIA: All right. She wants to be, she wants to be someone who is important to you. (*Now Virginia states a new positive intention for the mother, one that Linda is likely to welcome and accept, since Linda also wants to be important to her mother.*) Look what she picks. Your weight, your voice, and your musical talent. By any chance do you think you're too thin? (*Now Virginia is searching for points of agreement between Linda and her mother, with regard to the specific criticisms her mother makes, continuing to build her case for the similarity between them.*)

24:26   LINDA: I think I'm too thin, but (laughing) there isn't anything I can do about it. (*Linda totally ignores the point of agreement, so Virginia interrupts to bring her back to recognize it.*)

24:29   VIRGINIA: But wait a minute.

24:30   LINDA: Oh.

24:30   VIRGINIA: Wait a minute. [repetition]

24:31   LINDA: OK.

24:31   VIRGINIA: All right, so you join your mother, "Thank you. I have the same observation."

24:35   LINDA (laughing):   I will *not* say that to my mother! (*Although Linda refuses to say it, she is implicitly admitting that she agrees.*)

24:37   VIRGINIA: All right, go on being stubborn. (*Virginia presupposes that Linda has been stubborn. At this point it's enough that Linda admits her agreement to Virginia; she doesn't have to actually say it to her mother—which is something she objects to doing at this point.*) It's OK. And now about your voice. Does that ever get too loud? Have you ever noticed that for yourself?

24:47   LINDA: Yes, sure.

24:48   VIRGINIA: All right, so you say, "I notice the same thing." (*By saying, "So you say," Virginia is creating a situation that is close to Linda actually saying this to her mother. When Linda recalls it later, she may not remember whether she actually said it or not.*) Now, have you noticed that you have not been . . . ah . . . utilizing your music?"

24:59 LINDA: Maybe to what *she* would like. I feel like I use my music quite a lot.

25:03 VIRGINIA: OK, so you're in touch with your music in a way that she doesn't know about. (*This statement gently reframes her mother's criticism as "not knowing."* [meaning reframing]) Or if she knows about it, it doesn't fit what she would like. (*Virginia reframes disagreement as simply the result of different preferences.* [meaning reframing])

25:10 LINDA: Umhm.

25:11 VIRGINIA: Now, I notice you are giving me *lots* of resistance. (Linda laughs.) And that's typical, because it would be like if I—See, this is the game that people play. (*By using the general word "people," Virginia returns to speaking about Linda's issue in universal terms. She also presupposes that people are in the active role of playing a game. By using the word "game," what Linda is so concerned with is described as "not completely real."* [model of the world] Virginia lowers her voice.) And it's a *sad* game. And that is, I turn my parents into devils and saints.

25:25 LINDA: Umhm.

25:26 VIRGINIA: And if my parent (gesturing toward "mother") really cared about me, she would have dealt with me differently (gesturing back and forth between Linda and "mother") or he would have.

(*Although Virginia is speaking in general terms, her nonverbal gestures clearly indicate that she is talking about Linda and her mother. By talking in "quotes," as if Virginia were one of these "people," she makes it easy for Linda to think of this as a description of her situation—one which is the same as Virginia's earlier statement about her mother not believing that she was cared for* [23:33]. *This draws yet another parallel between Linda and her mother. The previous two minutes have been entirely devoted to pointing out similarities between Linda and her mother.*)

25:35 VIRGINIA: Now, what I'm—in a way I'm asking you to do a great big thing, which is to *respect* the fact that (reaching out to Linda's "mother's" shoulder and speaking softly) she grew up however she grew up. (*Calling what she is asking Linda to do "a great big thing" acknowledges the strength of Linda's objection. Virginia again turns Linda's attention to the "prior cause" of her mother's behavior—how she grew up.)*

25:44   LINDA (nodding):   Umhm.

25:45   VIRGINIA: She didn't grow up with any kinds of skills about how to be affectionate. She didn't know that. (Linda nods.) She didn't have anybody say to her (moving toward "mother" gently and touching her arm), "Oh, you're wonderful."

She got instead (harshly), "What are you doing that for?" (Virginia slaps "mother's" arm. Linda nods.) "Always disobeying. (Virginia raises her left arm sharply in a threatening gesture, as if preparing to strike, repeating this gesture after each of the next three sentences.) I'll clout you." (Linda nods.) "You'll probably come home pregnant in a few minutes." (Linda laughs.) I don't know. (softly) I mean, that's what she heard, OK?

(Virginia continues to reframe the mother's behavior—which Linda has thought of as resulting from bad intentions—as simply the result of the ignorance, incompetence, and confusion that resulted from a deficient upbringing. Acting this out makes it easier for Linda to see vividly what her mother's life must have been like, and makes it more likely that she will have an empathic response. After stating three examples in a serious tone, Virginia uses humor with the last example about "coming home pregnant in a few minutes.")

26:07   LINDA: Umhm.

26:08   VIRGINIA: Now . . . I'd just like you to be in touch (gestures in a long arc from Linda to her "mother") with whatever feelings that gets for you (*Virginia presupposes that it results in feelings*) to be now in touch with something about *her* inside. What is that? (*Virginia asks Linda to switch referential index with her mother in the scene Virginia has just created, and to notice her feelings as her mother: "be now in touch with something about her inside."*) What happens for you? (*Virginia presupposes that something happens.*)

26:24   LINDA (softly):   I think it—I'm really scared of feeling the depth of her pain. (Linda gestures toward her "mother," palm up. *Before, Linda saw her mother as being vindictive; now she presupposes "the depth of her pain."*)

26:29   VIRGINIA (nodding):   OK. I think that's a *very* important thing.

26:32   LINDA: Umhm.

26:33   VIRGINIA: That was true, and around you all the time. Your father couldn't do it, because it was too much; the pain was too strong. He also, also I think, did everything he could to make her life lighter. (*Virginia presupposes that Linda's father also felt pain, making him similar to her mother.*)

26:46   LINDA (nodding):   Umhm.

26:47   VIRGINIA: In *addition* to taking care of the kids. (Linda nods.) Also, at the same time, the behavior that came out of that was rejecting behavior—but not because *she* was rejecting. OK. But you couldn't know that. (*Now Virginia reframes Linda's old perception and response—in the past—as a reasonable response to lack of information.* [meaning reframing] *By saying, "You couldn't know that," in the past, Virginia presupposes that it is true, and that Linda can know it now.*)

26:59   LINDA (nodding):   Umhm.

27:00   VIRGINIA: When you're a little kid—would you get down on your knees to show that you are little? (*Linda kneels, giving her a perspective she has had only occasionally since she was a small child. This is a nonverbal invitation to become a small child again. Virginia lets go of Linda's hand that she has been holding.*) All right. And so she's coming out with her "education." (*Calling this "education" again implies a positive intention behind the mother's criticism.* Virginia points at Linda.) Your hair isn't right. (Virginia pushes Linda's left shoulder.) You've got to eat more. (Virginia pushes Linda's right shoulder.) You've got the wrong companions. (Virginia pushes Linda's left shoulder.) What else is it— Well, it doesn't even matter. You know what it is.

27:15   VIRGINIA: Now, your father comes along (drawing Linda's "father" toward Linda) and he—without making too big a fuss about it—kind of draws you over to him a little bit (Virginia pulls him closer and he puts his hand on Linda's shoulder. Linda, who is still kneeling, puts her arm around his waist.) and out of the sight of your mother, and you have something with him. Isn't that how it went? (*Throughout this description Virginia has used present tense, inviting Linda to associate into the past. Then she shifts from present to past tense in the last sentence.* [temporal predicate shift]))

27:29   LINDA (softly, smiling, in a "little" voice):   Yeah, he was nice.

27:31   VIRGINIA: He was nice. Yes. OK. You have to ask yourself, "How come, if he's so nice, how come she's such a devil?" But that's another question. (*Virginia issues a direct command to Linda—"You have to ask yourself" how it's possible for a devil to be married to a saint—and then brushes it aside with a hand gesture, so Linda is left with the question to consider, but without any opportunity or need to respond overtly. Right after Virginia says this, Linda— who has been looking directly at Virginia—looks away, up and to her right, for four seconds, blinks nine times, and smiles slightly, a strong indication that she is thinking about the question. In fact, the answer to Virginia's question is that it's not possible, so Linda's perceptions of her parents must be wrong.*)

27:38   VIRGINIA: All right, so at this moment in time, (Linda turns back to face Virginia) from the time you were very little, with the eyes that you had, you did exactly what you needed to do, because nobody was around. (*Virginia is amplifying her previous reframe that Linda's perceptions arose out of the limited understanding of a small child. This set of perceptions, described in past tense, is now associated with the kneeling position and with the past.*) You didn't come to this seminar yet, you know. (*By saying this, Virginia is presupposing that since Linda has come to the seminar, she can have new understandings.* Linda laughs.) And neither did your mother. (*Saying this presupposes that since Linda's mother didn't come to the seminar, she still can't achieve new understandings. Taken with the previous statement, the implication is that Linda is the only one who can change to improve her communication with her mother.*)

27:52   VIRGINIA: Now you are grown up, and it's like you took all of these learnings and you said in effect—Would you get up now? (Virginia reaches for Linda's right hand, gently pulls her up, and continues to hold her hand. *When Virginia says, "Now you are grown up," and pulls Linda to a standing position, this is an invitation to leave old childhood behavior behind. This is supported by Virginia's describing her childhood in past tense* [dissociation].) You said in effect "My mother did not find me acceptable. She did not find me lovable." (Linda keeps her hand on her "father's" lower back, while he moves his hand to her lower back. Virginia continues to hold Linda's right hand with her left, and speaks softly. *Virginia uses the word "find" with regard to Linda's being acceptable and lovable, which presupposes that she is acceptable and lovable.*)

28:08 VIRGINIA (harshly):   "And for *that* I will make her pay!" (Virginia looks intently at Linda and gestures almost in her face with a raised finger, repeatedly.) The revenge kind of thing that comes out of this. (*Virginia shifts to present tense when she describes the desire for revenge—as a result of the old childhood conclusions* [temporal predicate shift]. *As Virginia plays the role of Linda being vengeful, she does it directly to Linda, placing Linda in the position of receiving what Virginia is saying. The effect of this is to put Linda into her mother's shoes* [switch referential index]. Linda nods, and Virginia turns to the group.) How many of you know that one? "I'm going to make you pay!" (Virginia repeats her statement with the intensity and the finger gesture directed toward the group. Linda and the group laugh [normalization].) All right, I would—when you hear this, I don't want you to start doing a downer on yourself (Virginia turns back to Linda again), but the conclusions were that if you were—if she was any good, (softly) she would have *found* your lovability. (*Virginia begins the preceding sentence with present tense and then shifts to past tense when describing the old conclusions* [temporal predicate shift]. *By using the word "found," she presupposes Linda's lovability.*) All right. So now you are at a space, and what is she now, in her seventies? (*Getting her mother's age at this point creates a separation between the mother of Linda's childhood, who "deserves" revenge, and the mother of today, who is an old woman.*)

28:38 LINDA: Eighty-three.

28:39 VIRGINIA: Eighty-three. OK. She's still trying to find a way to be meaningful to you. (*By saying, "She's still . . . " Virginia presupposes the rest of the sentence.* Linda nods.) I don't want to push anything down your throat. (Linda nods.) What I am saying, it's like two kids that are battling in a family, and one wants to kill the other one. (Linda nods.) And one will say, "Listen, no matter what you do, *I'm not going to do it!* There! I'll kill you first." The one says, "Well, not unless I kill you first."

(*By using a metaphor of two kids, Virginia makes it easier for Linda to think about her situation lightly and in a dissociated way. This metaphor also contains a presupposition that the battle results from limited understanding, and feelings that are momentarily more intense than the situation warrants. Equality and symmetry are also presupposed in the story; no one is at fault.*)

29:04   VIRGINIA: All right (looking down left). What are we doing? We're talking about the vulnerability. (*By saying "the vulnerability" it is unclear whether Virginia is talking about Linda or her mother, thus reinforcing the similarity between them.*) And you still feel the *feeling* that she was rejecting you. (*By saying "still," Virginia presupposes that the feeling belongs to an earlier time, and also presupposes a distinction between feeling rejected and being rejected.* [model of the world] Linda nods.) Now, when I said to you, "Can you honor the fact that she noticed you?" that was hard. (*Virginia describes Linda's difficulty—"that was hard"—in past tense, inviting Linda to leave it in the past. Then Virginia shifts to present tense for the next task.* [temporal predicate shift]) I want you to ask her (Linda's "mother") a question, and you (Linda's "mother") answer however it comes out. "Have you ever loved and valued me?" (to Linda) Ask her about that. (*Virginia tries another approach to changing Linda's belief that her mother didn't care—asking "her" directly.*)

29:29   LINDA: Have you ever loved and valued me?

29:31   "MOTHER":   Yes, but I couldn't say so. (Linda nods.)

29:35   VIRGINIA (to Linda's "mother"):   Not only that. You had dreams that she could be what you were not. (Linda smiles.) Tell her about that. (*Virginia presupposes these dreams. She doesn't depend on the woman who is role-playing, but adds words she knows could be useful in changing Linda's belief.*)

29:44   "MOTHER":   I wanted all the things for you that I didn't have or couldn't have. (Linda nods.)

29:49   VIRGINIA (to Linda):   Do you believe that?

29:50   LINDA (nodding):   Umhm.

29:51   VIRGINIA (softly):   Come closer, just a step closer, (Linda steps closer to her "mother") while you let yourself believe that. (*Again Virginia links something that's easy—stepping closer—to something she wants to have happen with "while," which presupposes that what follows is true, and says "let yourself" to presuppose it will happen on its own.*) And she had what so many people of the world [have], a way of training and teaching which was (very softly), "How bad you are," and "Why aren't you different?" (*Virginia reemphasizes the mother's limited background as the reason for her critical behavior, and redescribes this as a "way of training and teaching."*) And I know you know a lot about that. (*This is ambiguous: it can mean both "You have experienced this from your mother," and "You have also done this."*) So as you look at her now, what are you feeling? (*This question is a way for Virginia to check how well her reframes and presuppositions have worked.*)

30:11   LINDA (beginning to cry):   Um, I'm feeling love.

30:14   VIRGINIA: OK.

30:15   LINDA: And sadness.

30:16   VIRGINIA (softly):   OK. Now what I'd like you to do is just be with that for a moment. (Linda nods) Because as you (a tear runs down Linda's cheek) *sense that feeling of love and sadness* [embedded command] (Linda nods), you begin to feel something different in here. (*Virginia gestures toward Linda's midsection. By saying "as you sense that feeling of love and sadness," Virginia presupposes that Linda will continue to sense these feelings and then links that— still by presupposition—with beginning to feel something different.*)

30:26   LINDA (nodding and closing her eyes):   Umhm.

30:29   VIRGINIA (*softly delivering what is essentially a hypnotic induction that continues to* [31:13]):   See, one of the things that saddens me so much, Linda, is how many people miss love in their lives (Linda nods) because there hasn't been anyone around to help them to discover it. (Linda nods. *Virginia is using a deliberate ambiguity; by saying "many people" she is talking about both Linda and her mother without overtly mentioning either. Thinking of love as something to discover presupposes that it's already there, waiting to be recognized. This is different from thinking of love as something you do, get, or give, for instance.)*

30:44   VIRGINIA (softly):   When we are little children, what we do is we do the best we can. (*Linda nods. Again, Virginia delivers the key presupposition that people do the best they can, and by using the inclusive "we"—four times—she is speaking simultaneously of herself, Linda, and her mother. This is easiest to verify by thinking of little kids, whose lack of understanding and limited background and abilities are so obvious. If a person really believes the presupposition that people always do the best they can, then there is no possibility of blame, anger, or resentment. When people behave badly, it's just something to be understood—and changed if possible, or avoided if it's not possible to change it.*)

30:50   VIRGINIA (softly):   Your mother, I can tell you, in a million years would never have *ever* thought that she was in any way discrediting you. (Linda nods.) She came out of an era of ignorance, and she came out of an era where she felt that she couldn't look at herself as of value. (Linda nods.) And she was following the same old "don't" pattern. (*Again Virginia makes the reframe that Linda's mother's critical behavior arose out of good intentions, but was blocked by ignorance and misconceptions.*)

31:13   LINDA (nodding):   Umhm.

31:15   VIRGINIA: So at this moment in time—Where is that husband of yours? Would you come and stand beside your mother-in-law? OK. What you said about him, "He's wonderful." I want you to look at him, and while you're thinking he's wonderful, would you out loud say, "I'm wonderful, too." See what happens to you. (*"I want you to look at him" is a simple request. "And" links this to the presupposition "while you're thinking he's wonderful," and to the following request to say to him, "I'm wonderful, too." "See what happens to you" focuses Linda's attention away from having to agree or disagree with the statement "I'm wonderful too," as well as from the request to say it out loud. Bringing up Linda's husband provides an opportunity to access some positive self-worth. Having him stand next to Linda's "mother" will help connect this wonderfulness to her also.*)

31:33   LINDA: I'm wonderful, too.

31:34   VIRGINIA: How did that feel to you?

31:36   LINDA (nodding):   It felt—wonderful. (Linda laughs.)

31:38   VIRGINIA: OK. Now, I want you to look at your mother, and know that if she knew what you know now, she could say the same thing. [switch referential index] (*Virginia uses "and" to link the simple task—"look at your mother"—with the presuppositions that follow. Previously Virginia had asked Linda to say "I'm wonderful," and Linda says it felt wonderful to say it. By saying, "What you know now," Virginia presupposes that Linda now knows more than she did earlier, and that is what made it possible for her to say, "I'm wonderful." This is an example of the assumption that, when people know better, they can change what they do. Virginia specifically presupposes that if Linda's mother had been through the seminar, she could be different. However, since Linda is the one going though the seminar, she is the one who can change. Linda nods.*) And what does that feel like for you?

31:52   LINDA: It's—(closing her eyes briefly) It's interesting. I feel like if I were to say some of the things that I really want to say to her (Linda's voice quavers)—both painful and wonderful—that that's very scary.

32:06   VIRGINIA (nodding):   Yeah, she would cry.

32:07   LINDA: Because it would unleash all of this emotion in her, because I've never seen her cry in my whole life, you know—that kind of thing.

32:11   VIRGINIA: And if she were to cry, can you bring a box of Kleenex along? (*Virginia reduces Linda's fear by using a humorous voice tone and a conversational postulate that gives her a simple and direct way of coping with her mother's tears. Linda nods.*) That's almost the only thing that happens when people cry—is they have tears. [repetition] (Linda laughs.) I've never see any building explode. (*Talking about a building exploding [exaggeration] puts Linda's catastrophic fears about the consequences of her mother expressing her feelings into perspective.*) And if you think there are going to be tears, I always think it's a kind, courteous, loving thing to do to bring Kleenex. (*Virginia again offers a simple, direct, specific way to deal with her mother's tears, described in a way that presupposes that the way to deal with tears is with kindness and love.)*

32:29 LINDA (nodding): Me too.

32:30 VIRGINIA: All right. So, now, as you look at her, and are able to connect with her and to talk to her about the things you found painful and wonderful, what does that feel like to you? (*By saying, "Now, as you look at her and . . . " Virginia presupposes that Linda is "able to connect with her and to talk to her about the things you found painful and wonderful . . . " and that Linda has feelings in response to that. In order to answer the question, "What does that feel like to you?" Linda has to do the rest of the instruction. Focusing Linda's attention on what comes afterwards tends to put her into the experience of doing it.)*

32:44 LINDA: *Very* scary. (*Since Linda has another objection, Virginia needs to back up and deal with it.)*

32:46 VIRGINIA: OK. All right. As you think about the scariness, what is the picture that comes to you? (*Virginia presupposes that a picture will come, and she gestures in the air to indicate a location for the picture. Virginia asks Linda for the picture she has, not about what her mother would do.* [model of the world]) The scariness. (Virginia gestures again in the air.) What picture are you seeing that makes it scary?

33:00 LINDA: The only—I don't see a picture, I just—I have a feeling of . . . just finally being that close to somebody. (*Linda states explicitly the connection between her difficulty with her mother and her initial wish to be able to connect and be close to others.* [0:22, 1:02])

33:10 VIRGINIA (nodding): OK.

33:10 LINDA: That vulnerability or that touching, (Virginia nods) or seeing my mother do something I've never seen her do before—express any emotion other than anger.

33:18 VIRGINIA (nodding): OK. All right.

33:19 LINDA: It's just scary.

33:20   VIRGINIA: OK. That's because it's *new*. (*Virginia reframes the fear as a response to the newness—not to some inherent danger.* [meaning reframing])

33:24   LINDA: Yes, in our relationship.

33:26   VIRGINIA: OK. Are the odds—and this takes at this moment in time—strong enough (*Virginia presupposes that the odds are strong at this moment in time*) for you to *risk seeing something new that you've never seen before?* [embedded command]

33:38   LINDA: I've asked myself that question a lot with—but only in terms of my mother. (*As Linda thinks about the question in relation to her mother, she is still reluctant, so Virginia changes the focus to Linda herself.*)

33:42   VIRGINIA: Well, let's see about *you,* because this has really to do with *you.* (*Again Virginia makes the distinction she made previously* [8:03, 15:48, 16:00, 32:46] *between the mother herself and Linda's images of her mother.* [model of the world])

33:47   LINDA: I am do—I feel that I am doing that—

33:49   VIRGINIA: Look at her now. (*If Linda is, in fact, doing something effective about her ability to connect with people, this will be evident in a role-play enactment. By saying, "Look at her now," Virginia is starting the process of testing this experientially.*)

33:50   LINDA: —in other relationships. I feel like I'm working out my relationship with my mother in other relationships.

33:56   VIRGINIA (firmly):   That will *not* be the same. Those people out there are not your mother. (gesturing toward Linda's "mother") This is your mother. (*Virginia knows that "working it out in other relationships" will not be nearly as valuable as resolving her resentment with the arch-enemy of her childhood. When Linda can come to resolution with her mother, this will generalize to all other close relationships.*)

34:05   VIRGINIA: You know what I have a hunch about? You don't want to lose. (Linda laughs.) And so you think if you start talking to your mother like this, she will have won. That's a *strong* feeling I have. Is there any value to that—validity? (*Virginia presents this as a hunch, treating Linda as the expert on her own feelings.*)

34:19   LINDA (hesitantly):   No, I'm not—I'm not—*feeling* that. (*Although Linda consciously disagrees, she unconsciously says "feeling" emphatically—while the rest of the sentence is hesitant and unsure, indicating that there is at least some truth in what Virginia suggested.*)

34:24   VIRGINIA: What are you feeling? (*Virginia easily accepts Linda's rejection of her hunch, and simply asks what Linda is feeling.*)

34:31   LINDA: I think I'm afraid to come out of hiding with my mother.

34:35   VIRGINIA: OK. Would you start off—let's do a little role play here and just see what happens. (*Virginia speaks to the group, inviting its participation in what is essentially a direct hypnotic induction full of generalities* [non-referring noun phrases], *spoken in a distinctly different tone and tempo, which is also directed at Linda.*) What I'm doing here, is I am *hoping* that what Linda is so beautifully allowing herself to do—the content may be painful but the process . . . . (*Virginia compliments Linda with the presupposed "beautifully allowing herself to do"*) We all have these things inside of ourselves in one way or another. And the process of allowing ourselves to *move in a different way* is what is being manifest here. (*Virginia presupposes that what is happening is "the process of allowing ourselves to move in a different way."* [embedded command] Virginia speaks to Linda again.) Remember where you came; you came from, "I feel power sometimes, and I feel wimpy sometimes." What I said [was] the wimpiness comes when you feel impotent. (*Notice that Virginia is still focused on the initial outcome.*)

35:11   LINDA: Umhm.

35:12   VIRGINIA: And what I gather in your mother, the impotence comes because you never really felt valued by her.

35:17   LINDA (nodding):   Umhm.

35:18   VIRGINIA: That's what I get, is that true?

35:20   LINDA: Yes. It might be an oversimplification in the sense that—

35:24 VIRGINIA: Most things are. (*Virginia's interruption stops Linda from becoming pointlessly analytical. The general statement also invites Linda to search for examples.*)

35:26 LINDA (smiling): OK.

35:27 VIRGINIA: Just like your attitude. Are you aware of that, too? (*Virginia first turns Linda's statement back onto Linda with a general statement, directly confronting her with the idea that her attitude is also an oversimplification. Virginia presupposes this. She doesn't ask Linda if it is true, but rather, "Are you aware of that?" The "too" includes the previous statement "Most things are" in what is presupposed.*)

35:30 VIRGINIA: I mean, the feeling (Linda nods) that she's ["mother"] going to vaporize, or, (Linda smiles) I don't know, you're going to vaporize. OK. (*This example is peripheral to the central issue, but it is one that Linda has to agree with because it's so overstated. Agreeing with this example will help Linda agree with the general statement. Linda was about to discount Virginia's summary of Linda's situation because it is an oversimplification. Instead, Virginia uses this to get Linda to discount her own oversimplification about the danger of connecting with her mother—a brilliant utilization.*)

35:35 LINDA (nodding): Umhm.

35:36 VIRGINIA (in a low, hypnotic tone and tempo): Because this belongs to a time when you were very little, and where you didn't have ways of looking at things. (*Again Virginia restates that Linda's response "belongs" to a past time when she had limited understanding—and by implication does not belong to the present, where she does have "ways of looking at things."*) The yearning piece inside of you—

35:52 VIRGINIA (gestures toward the group): Bring up your self-worth. Let's see what your self-worth is crying for. (Linda beckons to a woman who played the self-worth role for others earlier in the day.) And let's give somebody else a chance, because she's "self-worthed" out. (Linda laughs.) Look around and find somebody. It's OK. Anybody can do, male or female, or assorted."

36:10 LINDA (softly): Um, would you like to be my self-worth? (A woman comes up to be Linda's self-worth.)

36:19   VIRGINIA (to Linda's self-worth):   Would you get down behind, down below. (The woman kneels behind Linda. Virginia speaks again in a hypnotic tone and tempo.) And I—the song I've been hearing from there, with what you have been saying is, "I want to be loved and valued by everybody." Is that true or not true? (*Earlier* [35:56] *Virginia said, "Let's see what your self-worth is crying for," as if it were something to be discovered. However, Virginia specifies it. By posing the two categorical alternatives—"Is that true or not true?"—Virginia makes it hard for Linda to qualify her answer.*)

36:35   LINDA: That's true.

36:36   VIRGINIA (to Linda's self-worth):   So would you just start that way with just maybe a little—but just very lightly, "I want to be loved and valued by everyone."

36:42   LINDA'S "SELF-WORTH":   "I want to be loved and valued by everyone. (*Linda's "self-worth" continues to repeat this sentence softly and plaintively in the background until* [38:10]. *Having a voice repeat something softly behind you and below you is hypnotic, particularly when you have agreed that what the voice says is true of you. Linda's conscious attending and responding to what Virginia is saying adds to the hypnotic impact of the self-worth voice. There is very little difference between what Virginia is doing here and a double hypnotic induction, in which two people offer suggestions to a person simultaneously.*)

36:45   VIRGINIA (continuing in the low, slow hypnotic voice): Now there is a piece of you that says, "Be *careful*. You've got to be *careful* who you get to love and value you." (*By saying, ". . . who you get to love and value you," Virginia presupposes an active process.*) Is that not true? (*The last sentence, known as a "tag question," is a hypnotic technique used frequently by Milton Erickson. Asking a substantive question and following immediately with a tag question that negates the first question creates a fascinating ambiguity. Whatever Linda's response, it will be unclear whether it is a response to the substantive question or to the tag question. If she agrees, it will appear that she is agreeing to the first question. If she disagrees, it will appear that she is disagreeing with the tag question, and therefore agreeing with the first question.*)

36:52   LINDA: Umhm.

36:53   VIRGINIA: All right. Now, could you for the moment allow yourself to know that you need to be cautious, but that you don't have to have your caution in *front* of you (gesturing in front of Linda); you can have it *beside* you (gesturing to Linda's right side). (*By saying, "Allow yourself to know . . . " the rest of the sentence becomes presupposed. The implication is that Linda can continue to be cautious, yet in a way that doesn't interfere with her connecting with others. By first gesturing in front of Linda and then gesturing with a pushing motion off to her side, Virginia literally moves Linda's image of caution out of her way, where it won't inhibit her.*)

37:08   VIRGINIA (still speaking hypnotically):   And that you can go into another place in yourself where you *know* something about this lady (Virginia gestures toward Linda's "mother.") as a human being, that the way she is has very little to do with you. (*In this last sentence, everything after the word "go" is presupposed. The most important part is the repetition of " . . . the way she is has very little to do with you." If all the mother's behavior is simply a result of her background and has little to do with Linda, that changes the entire meaning of the mother's behavior.* [meaning reframing]) You know that. (*This presupposes that all the foregoing is true. There are four layers of presupposition here, nested inside each other. At the center is the central issue: "the way she is has very little to do with you." This is presupposed within " . . . another place in yourself where you know something about this lady," which in turn is presupposed as a place that Linda can go. The final "You know that" presupposes everything else. Nested presuppositions are particularly hard to recognize and unravel, so they have greater impact.*)

37:23   LINDA (nodding):   Umhm.

37:24   VIRGINIA: I think a piece of you does know that. (*This statement is hard to dispute without checking thoroughly with every "piece" of yourself! And even if you did, and no part knew it, the sentence still presupposes that it is true.*)

37:25   LINDA (nodding):   Umhm.

37:26   VIRGINIA: But the hurt that's gone on for so many years—You want to see the dancing in her eyes. (*First Virginia mentions the unpleasant past and then poses an attractive future, stated as a desire in the present.* [temporal predicate shift] *This sets up a situation that is strongly motivating: away from pain and toward pleasure. Since Linda has not said anything about wanting to see her mother happy, this is straight hypnotic induction—inducing the kinds of feelings Virginia wants Linda to have.*) And you are still leaving it all up to her. (*"Still" presupposes that Linda has been leaving it up to her mother.*) And it would be nice. (*Although it would be nice if her mother changed, as long as Linda insists that her mother must be the one to change, the situation remains out of her control, and Linda will feel impotent and vulnerable. Next Virginia will gently suggest that Linda could be the person who initiates change. She does this by presupposing that Linda now has the knowledge and abilities to do this, which her mother still lacks. This was foreshadowed earlier* [27:48, 31:38].)

37:37 VIRGINIA: But, what about for *you,* starting a process she knows nothing about? What about you *being* that child that's grown up now, who can manage on new things, because you've learned new things? (*Virginia states a straight cause-effect. "You can do new things because you have learned new things."*) Your mother isn't here.

37:52 LINDA: Umhm.

37:53 VIRGINIA: She wouldn't know how to do this. (*Again the implication is that since her mother isn't able to improve the communication, it's up to Linda to do it. This statement, and the earlier "she knows nothing about"* [37:37] *gives Linda another way to "win" with her mother* [33:53]. *She can win by moving on and changing in ways her mother wouldn't be able to do.*) Could you show her the way?

37:58 LINDA: I'd like to.

37:59 VIRGINIA (continuing in the hypnotic voice): Look at her, and let that be part of what you are in touch with now. (*"Look at her, and . . ." links a simple action with what follows, indicating that it will be just as easy as the looking. "And let that be . . . " presupposes the rest of the sentence. By saying "part of," Virginia presupposes that Linda will also be in touch with other things.*) And know that showing her the way might begin to give some response for this little self-worth, "I want to be loved and valued." (*"And" links the sentence to the preceding one, and "know that . . . " presupposes the rest of the sentence—that if Linda did this it would give her some of the positive response that her self-worth has been yearning for for so long. Linda's self-worth stops saying her sentence, but stays in her kneeling position behind Linda.*) What does that feel like to you? (*To answer the question, "What does that feel like to you?" Linda has to complete Virginia's presupposed instructions.*)

38:20   LINDA (softly):   I'm willing. I've been looking . . . . for that way. (*Linda is expressing congruent willingness. However, by saying she has "been looking . . . for that way" she also indicates that she still doesn't see what to do—even though Virginia has shown her before—so Virginia proceeds to demonstrate to Linda in more detail what she can do.*)

38:25   VIRGINIA (nodding):   OK. Now, what I would like you to do now, and see what it sounds like. (*Linda says she's been "looking," so Virginia will give her a detailed picture. "See what it sounds like" is an explicit instruction to listen to Virginia's words and make pictures of their meaning. Virginia then demonstrates exactly what she wants Linda to do. Notice that although Virginia is doing all the communicating with Linda's "mother," she introduces it by saying, "What I would like you to do now . . . " So even though Virginia is actually doing it, it's framed as if Linda herself is doing it. Virginia turns to Linda's "mother" and speaks softly to her, in "quotes," as if Virginia were Linda.*)

38:28   VIRGINIA: "Thank you for paying attention to me. And there are some things in the way you pay attention that I would like to share with you that don't fit with me." And going up to her and taking her hand when you thank her. (Virginia reaches out to take "mother's" hand.) Because that's the piece (Virginia turns toward Linda) that she needs. The piece that you want to do is to share how you are different from what she expects you to be. (*Virginia makes a distinction between what her mother needs to hear—appreciation for her efforts and good intentions—and what Linda needs to express—her differentness and individuality. Virginia turns to Linda's "mother."*) So that you can say, "You know, I've been worried about my weight, too. I can't seem to gain any weight." Or, "I've been worried sometimes when I talk too loud. I share those. The music is another thing, because I do it differently."

(When Virginia previously asked Linda to express appreciation for her mother, she couldn't do it because it was too big a chunk of new behavior which was inconsistent with Linda's perceptions and feelings. Now Linda has different perceptions and feelings of willingness that will support new behavior. However, to be sure that Linda can do it, Virginia simplifies the task by giving a complete demonstration of what to do—the words to say, the posture, voice tone, gestures, etc. that go with it. This gives Linda the way she has been looking for.)

39:00 VIRGINIA: Could you imagine yourself doing that? *(Before asking Linda to do what Virginia has just demonstrated, she asks if she can imagine herself doing it.)*

39:03 LINDA (nodding):   Umhm.

39:04 VIRGINIA: Now. *(By asking, "Could you imagine yourself doing that?" [39:00] waiting for Linda's agreement, and then adding the word "now," Virginia gracefully modifies what Linda agreed to—from "imagining doing it," to "imagining doing it now.")* Let's see what happens as you move it out of your throat. *(Virginia presupposes that Linda will move it out of her throat, focusing her attention on "seeing what happens" when she does it.)*

39:10 LINDA (hesitates, smiles, and then steps up to her "mother" and takes both her hands in hers):   Mom, I really appreciate . . . you . . . noticing me, but I need to tell you a couple of things about me.

39:18 VIRGINIA: Would you leave the "but" off, and let that be a complete sentence by itself. *(Fritz Perls used to call the word "but" a "killer" because it negates everything that precedes it in a sentence. To discover how this works in your own experience, make up a sentence with "but" in it, and notice how your image of the first part of the sentence disappears or is cancelled. As Linda tries out the new behavior, Virginia can notice and adjust anything that might interfere with clear communication with her mother.)*

39:22 LINDA: OK. (hesitating) Mom, (smiling) I really appreciate . . . you noticing me. The thing with the weight has come up nine thousand four hundred and eighty-three times—(Linda turns to Virginia) No, I'm just kidding. (The group laughs, and Linda turns back to her mother.) The thing with the weight has come up so often, and I need you to know that I feel healthy, vibrant. I am not sick. You know—you *know* how I live. I eat good food. I exercise all the time, and I see that you are worried about me, and I would just like to suggest that you not worry anymore, because I am really healthy. (Linda's voice still sounds a little defensive and resentful.)

40:00 VIRGINIA: All right, now let this stay for a moment and just get in touch with how you are feeling about sharing this delicate truthful part of yourself with your mother, in a context of acknowledging her presence as well. (*Everything after "sharing" is presupposed, creating an important frame of mutual acknowledgement. Linda wants her mother to acknowledge her; Virginia also wants Linda to acknowledge her mother.*) How does that feel?

40:16 LINDA: It feels . . . schizophrenic. One part of me feels really wonderful in doing that, and the other part of me is going like this (Linda pantomimes, guarding her stomach with her left hand, and as if warding off a blow to her head with her right hand.) waiting for her to come back and say, "But you look *terrible*. You're skinny and, you know, you're never going to have any friends if you are that skinny."

40:31 VIRGINIA: OK. All right, now we have to stop at this moment. (*The session has gone well into the lunch hour, and to the end of the videotape. Linda has made several major shifts, and there is more to do.*) And I would like to start with that after the lunch, (Linda laughs) because this is also another *wonderful* piece. (*Virginia presupposes that what Linda has already done is wonderful, by calling Linda's ambivalence "another wonderful piece." This also makes it more inviting to continue after lunch.*) Are you game for doing that?

40:40 LINDA: Yes.

40:41 VIRGINIA: All right, so let us stop here, right now, and then we can go on with this after the lunch. OK?

40:46 LINDA: OK.

40:47 VIRGINIA: Thank you. (The group applauds, and Linda and the others on the stage turn to rejoin the group.) Linda, Linda, come back. (Virginia reaches out to Linda, and they hug each other.)

(LUNCH BREAK)

40:50 VIRGINIA: Linda, would you come back? (to the group) You see, there are a couple of things when I move as I was moving this morning— (As Linda steps up to be with Virginia, Virginia takes her hand and holds it.) Hello, love.

40:57 LINDA: Hi.

40:58 VIRGINIA: —and that is, I would not want to exploit anybody. I don't want to leave anybody hanging. (Virginia turns to speak to Linda.) When we start something, the process of change is one that we need to move through with it. And the last thing I would want you to do, to remember from this morning, is that you *had* to do anything different. (*Virginia states what she doesn't want. Next she uses the word "but" to cancel it out, and follows with positive possibilities.*) But if something changed or appealed to you, or you wanted to move out somehow or another with getting some new perspectives on things, then some things would happen. (*This is an "if-then," cause-effect sentence that presupposes that "some things would happen" if Linda experienced any of the things mentioned in the first part of the sentence.*) So I wondered what *did* happen for you . . . after we left—after you left the stage. [embedded question]

41:33 LINDA (her soft tonality is different from before lunch): I felt . . . I *feel* . . . incomplete. Um . . . lots of fear about whatever it is I am trying to let go, or transform into love, or however you want to say it. I felt spacy at some point and I felt tired at other points, and then I felt weak-kneed at other points, but I *really* want to *finish it*. (*"Really . . . finish it" is an embedded command directed toward Virginia!*)

42:01   VIRGINIA: OK. Now, do you have in your mind an image of what "finished" means? When you have finished, how will you know you have finished? (*These are important questions that many therapists never ask. In the more general case, the questions are, "What do you want?"—outcome—and, "How will you know when you have it?"—the sensory-based evidence that lets you know you have achieved it. In this case, Virginia asks Linda to do this visually, by asking for an image.* Then Virginia turns to the group.) By the way, would your mother come and stand behind me? Where is she? There she is. Just stand behind me, and with your (Linda's) father, too. (to Linda's "mother") Find your husband. Just behind me, now, while you (Linda) talk to me about what would it look like when you were finished. (*"While" presupposes the rest of the sentence.* As Linda's "mother" and "father" come up on stage and stand behind Virginia, she turns to face Linda directly and takes both Linda's hands in hers.) This is the question a lot of people will ask.

42:24   LINDA: I see it in terms of layers. I guess some sort of clarity.

42:30   VIRGINIA: What is the clarity about? (*Virginia asks for more specific information.*)

42:33   LINDA: About what I can do . . . to . . . "click over" to a different mode of communicating with my mother.

42:44   VIRGINIA: Do you want to do that? (*Virginia asks about her motivation and commitment to this goal.*)

42:45   LINDA (hesitantly):   I *think* so.

42:46   VIRGINIA: All right. Check inside and see if there is any objection to what you are saying right now, any objection at all. (*Since Linda has expressed ambivalence, there is probably an objection, which must be dealt with before Linda can proceed congruently toward the outcome.*)

42:57   LINDA: Well, the objection comes up (shaking her head) in the fear again, of—

43:02   VIRGINIA: All right, would you give me a picture of the fear, *your* picture of the fear? (*Linda's objection was a feeling of fear. Virginia asks for the picture that gives rise to the fear, and emphasizes that it's Linda's picture—in contrast to the possible events in the world she's afraid of.* [model of the world] *This picture will provide more detailed information about what Linda is afraid of than the feeling.*) Let's see what we can do with that. (*"What we can do" presupposes that something can be done.*)

43:08   LINDA: OK, my picture of the fear is . . . um . . . opening up communication with my mother so that either I say or she says—that we say things to each other that would be very . . . hurting. Sometimes I think I'm afraid that if I really communicated with my mother, that this dam would break, and I would say everything I've ever wanted to say to her that was painful.

43:37   VIRGINIA: OK. I think I'm getting a sense of something about what you are talking about. That in your quest for getting a new connection with your mother (*Virginia presupposes that "getting a new connection with your mother" is Linda's quest*), the fear is—and it might be justified—that you will make things worse. (*By acknowledging that Linda's fear "might be justified," Virginia is also gently presupposing that it also might not be justified. She also redescribes Linda's fear of saying painful things as "making things worse"* [meaning reframing], *which presupposes that the present situation, which Linda has been clinging to tenaciously, is bad.*)

43:56   LINDA (nodding):   Umhm.

43:57   VIRGINIA: All right. Now, are you aware that you really don't have this to say to your mother, but you have this to say to your *image* of your mother? (*This is a crucial distinction that provides a way of dealing with Linda's objection. By presupposing that the conflict is within Linda—and not between her and her actual mother—Virginia allows Linda to say anything in Virginia's presence, without risking the response she fears she might get from her actual mother. This was foreshadowed earlier* [8:03, 11:25, 15:48, 16:00, 32:46, 33:42, 43:02]. *Virginia kept making essential reframes like this over and over until the client accepted them.*)

44:05   LINDA: Intellectually I know that. I can't seem to bring that through.

44:11   VIRGINIA: OK. Now, we may not do that today. We may not do that today. [repetition] (*By saying, "We may not do that today," Virginia presupposes that it's possible to do it—even today. She is also essentially saying, "I don't need you to do this—I won't push you to do this. If you want it, you'll need to do it yourself." Backing off in this way with someone who has raised a lot of objections can be a useful way to reactivate a person's motivation. It is also a way to be sure Virginia avoids a trap that many therapists fall into—working much harder on an outcome than the client does.)* Because one of the things I sense about you is you have a highly developed ability to stand firm on things. [meaning reframing] (Linda laughs) That could sometimes be misunderstood as—

44:23   LINDA (smiling):   That's called "stubborn."

44:25   VIRGINIA: Yes. Well it could be, yes. I didn't say that, it was—

44:27   LINDA: That was very nice, Virginia. (Linda and the group laugh. *Even though Linda recognizes Virginia's reframe, and laughs at it, it still has a positive effect on how Linda views this behavior.*)

44:31   VIRGINIA: And that there is a longstanding business about this—of this worry, and the last thing you want to do is to isolate you and your mother more. (*Initially Linda's fear was that she might "say everything I've ever wanted to say to her that was painful," focusing on possible unpleasant consequences [43:08]. Virginia earlier redescribed this as "making things worse" [43:54] presupposing that the present situation is bad. Now she redescribes Linda's fear as the fear that she might "isolate you and your mother more." The word "more" presupposes that Linda and her mother are isolated already. Although the different meanings are similar, thinking of the fear in terms of possibly saying things that are painful will tend to make Linda avoid communicating; thinking about avoiding a bad situation and further isolation will be likely to motivate Linda toward communication rather than away from it. What began as an objection to communication has become a reason to proceed.* [meaning reframing])

44:39   LINDA (nodding):   Umhm.

44:40   VIRGINIA: That's what I get. OK. Now, I'm going to tell you something from my head to your head (*Virginia gestures from her head to Linda's lower chest. "I'm going to tell you something*

*from my head to your head" is an interesting communication, partic-
ularly when Virginia gestures toward her own head, but does not gesture toward Linda's head. In effect it says, "I'm not talking to you;
someone else is talking to someone else," inviting Linda to wonder
who is talking to who. By saying "my head" and "your head,"
Virginia is literally saying, "a part of me is telling something to a
part of you." Ericksonians would say, "My unconscious is telling your
unconscious," which is a direct hypnotic communication.)* and I don't
know whether you will agree with it, and that's all right. *(By saying
this, Virginia is saying, in effect, "This is not a conscious communication, so it doesn't matter if you agree with it or not.")*

44:49   VIRGINIA: I'm going to ask that (Virginia picks up a
pillow and holds it across her chest) this pillow represent all of your
infantile angers (Linda laughs) right here. *(By saying, "I'm going to
ask," Virginia gracefully avoids the question of whether it's true or not,
creating an "as if" or "pretend" quality in what she does next. She
also presupposes that Linda's anger is infantile.* Linda laughs.)

45:00   VIRGINIA: And I want you to talk to this pillow about
all the *things* that you've wanted to *say* (*"things . . . say" is equivalent
to "say things," a special form of embedded command based on childhood "pivot grammar." When children first learn to speak more than
one word at a time, they experiment with linking verbs and things—
"Baby go," "Food eat"—before they learn the grammatical sequence
of subject, verb, object.)* to this person back here (Virginia gestures
toward Linda's "mother"), but it's really this (gesturing toward the
pillow). And I want you to see what happens when you start to say
that. *(Virginia again uses "see what happens when . . ." to presuppose
Linda's starting to do what she asks.)* I will not be hurt by this, but—
and neither will this pillow. *(First Virginia creates a situation that is
separate from Linda's mother, to avoid Linda's objection that she
might hurt her mother with what she might say. To make it even safer
for Linda, Virginia points out that she won't be hurt by whatever
Linda says, and humorously adds that "neither will this pillow" be
hurt.)*

45:16   LINDA: This is called crying in front of eight million
people. *(Again we hear Linda's talent for exaggeration, which, as
usual, Virginia will challenge immediately.)*

45:19   VIRGINIA (looking out at the group):   Eight million? (The group laughs.) You don't count very well.

45:21   LINDA (gesturing toward Helen, who arranged for the weekend and the videotaping):   Helen sells a lot of tapes. (The group laughs.)

45:24   VIRGINIA: Well, she may not put you on [videotape]. Will that be disappointing to you? (*By saying this, Virginia is jokingly and indirectly suggesting that there could also be an opposite response in Linda—a response of wanting to be seen.*)

45:27   LINDA: Oh, maybe.

45:28   VIRGINIA: All right. See, what this would be in a universal—in a universal, Linda—

45:34   LINDA: (smiling):   Uh huh.

45:35   VIRGINIA: —is what we bring up as children, we carry into life as adults, unless we integrate it. (*Since Linda has brought up the audience, and possible embarrassment, Virginia returns to the universal level of how it is healing for all of us to do what Linda is doing. This makes Linda the same as her audience, eliminating the possibility of embarrassment.*)

45:41   LINDA: Right.

45:42   VIRGINIA: And I can't think of something that would be more healing to people—(*Linda's concern about crying in public is redescribed as "something that would be more healing to people."*)

45:47   LINDA: Umhm.

45:48   VIRGINIA: —both on the level of "I know about that" and also on this other wonderful level, because your caring (*Virginia presupposes Linda's caring*) is so much out in front (*"So much" presupposes the caring is "out in front." Linda nods.*) that actually you know that this really has very little to do with your mother at this time. (*By saying, ". . . actually you know that . . . " the rest of the sentence is presupposed, reiterating the theme that the conflict is actually within Linda, not between her and her mother* [43:57]. *"At this time" separates the present from an earlier time when the conflict was actually with her mother.*)

46:00 LINDA: Umhm.

46:01 VIRGINIA: As a matter of fact, probably you realize that if you were to say these things to your mother, she would say, "I don't remember that." (*By saying "probably you realize that . . ." the rest of the sentence is gracefully presupposed to be true.*)

46:08 LINDA (nodding): Umhm.

46:09 VIRGINIA: Can you know that's true? (*The conversational postulate again presupposes "that"—the preceding comment— is true.*)

46:10 LINDA: (nodding): Umhm.

46:11 VIRGINIA: So that actually in a way we're beating up somebody, but somehow sometimes things *stick* in our craw, and sometimes the release—it's the release out of here (gesturing toward her own chest and neck) that we need to get at. (*Virginia again describes this as a universal process—something we all do and can benefit from—to make it easier for Linda to do.*) So, what would you tell . . . here is this image of your mother, what would you tell? (*Again Virginia specifies that this is the image, not the mother herself* [model of the world], *and presupposes that Linda will tell her mother something.*)

46:29 LINDA: Um (beginning to cry), I want to tell her that—

46:33 VIRGINIA: Say "you" to her. (*By talking about her mother as "her," Linda can still stay dissociated from her feelings. When Virginia asks Linda to say "you," the encounter with her mother becomes more immediate and present, and Linda's feelings will become fuller.* [association])

46:43 LINDA: OK. (closing her eyes briefly, and sighing) That you really *hurt* me (Linda cries) being unable to . . . (shaking her head back and forth) ever tell me that you loved me, ever . . . nurture me, tuck me in at night, bathe me. Just the simple things that mothers do, you avoided (with both hands in a pushing gesture) just because you didn't—you couldn't be intimate. (*Here Linda says that her mother's inadequate parenting resulted from inability, rather than the bad intentions she mentioned earlier* [15:52], *an important shift. Linda is expressing an extreme generalization about her mother—*

that she never ever did any of these loving things—an important gen-
eralization to challenge.)

47:10 VIRGINIA: OK, now I would like you to close your eyes, and I'm going to take your hand, and I'm going to imagine you ten days old. (*When Virginia says, "I'm going to imagine you ten days old," she indirectly invites Linda to age regress.*) Who's bathing you? (*Virginia presupposes that someone is bathing her.*)

47:17 LINDA (shaking her head and rejecting the presupposition):   No one.

47:18 VIRGINIA: No one? You go dirty?

47:19 LINDA: Umhm.

47:20 VIRGINIA: I don't believe it. [direct challenge] Do you believe it?

47:22 LINDA (shaking her head side to side):   I do.

47:23 VIRGINIA: How dirty were you when you got your first bath? Six years old? (*By asking an extreme question—yet one that embodies a logical possibility, given what Linda has said—Linda will have to clarify and correct what she said. Virginia could simply have asked, "How old were you when you got your first bath?" By asking, "How dirty were you when you got your first bath? Six years old?" she creates a more vivid and extreme picture of the unlikeliness of what Linda has said.*)

47:27 LINDA: Oh! (laughs) Maybe somebody was bathing me. Maybe she bathed me when I was ten days old.

47:31 VIRGINIA: All right, now I want you to keep your eyes closed.

47:34 LINDA: OK.

47:35 VIRGINIA: And I want you to go inside and (skeptically) see if you really buy *that*—that you didn't get any baths from anybody until you were ten days old.

47:56 LINDA (after a pause of eleven seconds):   Possibly (nodding).

47:57 VIRGINIA: Possibly.

47:58   LINDA: Umhm.

47:59   VIRGINIA: Possibly what?

48:01   LINDA: I didn't get a bath until I was ten days old.

48:03   VIRGINIA: Now what I—all of a sudden—am in touch with is leprosy. Is that what you're talking about, that your mother couldn't touch you because you had leprosy or something like that? (*Virginia makes Linda's extreme statement even more extreme, in order to make it seem even more ridiculous.* [exaggeration])

48:14   LINDA: No, it wasn't me, it was *her.*

48:17   VIRGINIA: *She* had leprosy? (*Virginia is perhaps being obtuse deliberately.*)

48:18   LINDA: No, she couldn't touch me.

48:20   VIRGINIA: Why?

48:21   LINDA: Because she was terrified of me. (*Here Linda states a new cause-effect: fear causes her mother's inadequate behavior.*)

48:22   VIRGINIA: And you were how old, and how big?

48:25   LINDA (with feeling):   I was a *wonderful* little baby.

48:28   VIRGINIA (challenging):   "Wonderful little baby." Where did you get that idea? (*It may seem strange that Virginia challenges Linda's assertion that she "was a wonderful little baby." However, this is the flip side of Linda's blaming her mother for everything. If the baby is totally wonderful, then everything that went wrong was the mother's fault.*)

48:30   LINDA: I *know* I was. (Linda begins to cry. *She reasserts what she has said even more strongly, so Virginia uses this.*)

48:32   VIRGINIA (softly):   All right, now I would like you to look up at me, and let yourself *see* that wonderful part, that you are this wonderful little baby. (*Virginia uses "and" to link the easy task— "look up at me"—with the presuppositions that follow, introduced by "let yourself." Linda said, "I was a wonderful little baby" [48:25]. Virginia changes this to present tense, "You are this wonderful little baby," to add to Linda's self-worth. Linda nods.*) Your mother knew that, too. (Linda nods.) Your mother knew that, too. [repetition] Do you know that she did? [presupposition]

48:44 LINDA (crying, with resentment): I know that she did; I know that she didn't put it out. (She gestures with her right hand, palm up, in a hitting motion toward her mother in the same way as earlier [8:12]. *Linda now accepts that her mother knew Linda was wonderful.*)

48:48 VIRGINIA: Oh, OK. So how long now are you going to trouble yourself and make yourself feel bad for somebody who had it inside, but couldn't put it out? How long are you going to do that for you? (*By asking, "How long are you going to . . ." Virginia presupposes that what she says in the rest of the sentence has been going on—that Linda has been actively troubling herself and making herself feel bad, and that it is her choice whether to continue or not. This is very different from Linda blaming her mother for her troubles.*)

49:00 LINDA (still crying): I . . . I'm looking, I'd like to . . . end it . . . right now . . . if I could.

49:06 VIRGINIA: Is there any part of you that does not fully believe that your mother was *very, very* connected with you and cared *very* much about you? (*By asking, "Is there any part of you that does not fully believe that . . . " the rest of the sentence is presupposed— that her mother was connected and cared very much, and that all the other parts of Linda believe this.*) In fact, was *so* careful and cared *so much* that she almost nagged you? (*Virginia has posed a new cause-effect that changes the meaning of Linda's mother's nagging. Now the nagging was the result of her mother's caring so much. Before Linda thought the nagging meant that her mother hated her [15:57]. [meaning reframing]*) Is there any question—

49:21 LINDA (resentfully): Not *almost,* Virginia.

49:23 VIRGINIA: She *did* nag you. All right, then I'll make it very strong, that she nagged you. She cared about you so much she nagged you. (*Virginia uses Linda's objection to add even stronger support for the new cause-effect that presupposes Linda's mother's caring.*)

49:28 LINDA (nodding): Umhm.

49:29   VIRGINIA: OK. Now, you know that to be true? (*Virginia is presupposing that it is true.*)

49:34   LINDA (thoughtfully):   I think I do. (*Since Linda has expressed uncertainty—"I think I do" is very different from "I do"— Virginia asks Linda to check again for objections.*)

49:36   VIRGINIA: All right, go inside and see if there is any objection, love— (Linda closes her eyes) that any part of your body thinks that there's an objection to what you're saying. (*Since uncon-scious objections are often manifested as physical feelings of tension, discomfort, etc., Virginia asks Linda to pay attention to all parts of her body. By saying " . . . any part of your body thinks there is an objec-tion," Virginia leaves open the possibility that an objecting part doesn't really object, it only thinks it does* [model of the world]*—and that all other parts do not have objections.*)

49:50   LINDA: There's some—(Linda shakes her head) there's something, but I don't know what it is.

49:56   VIRGINIA: What does it feel like? (to Linda's "self-worth") Your little self-worth, would you come back here? We need you. (Linda's self-worth comes up and kneels behind Linda. *Virginia does not use Linda's self-worth until more than sixteen minutes later* [66:19]*, another indication of her planning the course of the session.*)

50:02   LINDA: It feels like—the sense I've had all my life is that . . . . part of her loved me beyond belief, and part of her wanted to destroy me. (*Again, Linda expresses a polarity of extreme opposites, one of which is that her mother loved her very much, which Virginia has just presupposed* [49:06].)

50:17   VIRGINIA: All right, let's take that—both parts. "She loved you beyond belief." (*Virginia takes the positive part first.*)

50:20   LINDA: Right.

50:21   VIRGINIA: What part of her was that part?

50:26   LINDA (very softly):   I guess her heart, and whatever a mother . . . something very deep.

50:31   VIRGINIA: Would you pick out your mother's heart, please, from out of the audience?

50:43   LINDA (scanning the group, smiling):   Bruce. (Bruce comes up and stands to Linda's right.)

50:46   VIRGINIA: All right, this is your mother's heart.

50:48   LINDA (laughing):   Believe it or not!

50:50   VIRGINIA: Yes, she has a wonderful heart.

50:51   LINDA (with feeling):   She does.

50:52   VIRGINIA (to Bruce):   All right, you just be here. Now, what part of you do you think is your mother's destruction of you?

51:00   LINDA: What part of her?

51:02   VIRGINIA: Umhm.

51:06   LINDA: Her . . . her upbringing. (*Linda's focus on her mother's upbringing as a cause of the negative behavior is probably the result of Virginia's earlier work* [25:45, 27:00, 27:38, 29:51, 30:50, 37:08].)

51:10   VIRGINIA: Would you bring her upbringing, please? (gesturing toward the group) And do that in the form of her father and her mother. Did she have any brothers or sisters?

51:18   LINDA: Seven.

51:20   VIRGINIA: Seven brothers and sisters? All right, find a mother and a father and seven brothers and sisters, and we will put them around here somewhere. (*The next couple of minutes—to* [53:03]—*are taken up with picking out people to play the roles of Linda's mother's family.*)

51:24   LINDA: OK.

51:28   VIRGINIA: As a matter of fact, we will move down here. (She moves off a "riser" to a lower level to provide more space for the family.) Let all the parts move down here.

51:33   LINDA: You can be my mother's mother, Marcie.

51:35   VIRGINIA: That's your grandmother, if you don't mind. Yes, your mother's mother, Marcie. OK, would you come up here and bring your father up here?

51:40   LINDA: Would you come up to be my grandfather?

51:46   VIRGINIA: OK. Would you be right over here (to Virginia's right), now, on this side right there?

51:50   LINDA: I think one of her brothers died.

51:52   VIRGINIA: That doesn't matter; he left his imprint behind.

51:54   LINDA: Would you come up, would—just all of you come up?

51:56   VIRGINIA: Are they all . . .would they—? Let's not fiddle with the genitals if we can help it. (The group laughs.)

52:01   LINDA: OK. You mean, let's make them all what they were?

52:04   VIRGINIA: Yes. That's what "fiddling" means.

52:08   LINDA: Three sisters.

52:10   VIRGINIA: And four brothers? Or three brothers?

52:13   LINDA: And three brothers.

52:14   VIRGINIA: Because you were one of those. Will you pick a stand-in for yourself? No, wait a minute, not you. Of course not. This belongs to somebody else. (*Virginia has momentarily jumped ahead to the time* [62:26] *when she will ask Linda to pick a stand-in for herself—another indication that she has a clear plan for how to assist Linda in reaching resolution.*)

52:19   LINDA: My mother's already here.

52:20   VIRGINIA: Your mother's already here, so we got her.

52:22   LINDA: We need three men.

52:24   VIRGINIA: Three men, OK, so we want to find some . . . here's one.

52:27   LINDA: One, and—Do you two guys want to come up and—

52:29   VIRGINIA: There are two of them back against the wall. I think so, come on up.

52:31   LINDA: OK, you have to leave? OK.

52:33 VIRGINIA: Well, we aren't going to be that long, but how many—how long are you both going to be here? Let's see if we can get that. Fine, thank you. Are you going to be here? Oh, there's one right there.

52:44 LINDA: Oh, yeah, come on up, please.

52:46 VIRGINIA: They're sparse, but they are here.

52:47 "MOTHER'S HEART": Is it OK for me to be her mother's heart?

52:50 VIRGINIA: Yes, of course it's all right. Hearts have no sex, by the way. (laughter) There's no such thing as a woman's heart and a man's heart. Heart is heart. All right. This now—here's your mother.

53:02 LINDA: Right.

53:03 VIRGINIA: And what you said is the part of her that wants to destroy you is represented by all these (gesturing to mother's family).

53:08 LINDA: Umhm.

53:10 VIRGINIA: OK, now when you say that, what you are also saying is the conclusions that she ("mother") reached—however she reached them—about what happened here (in her family), was the part that got in her way of having her heart talk to you—is what you're telling me. (*This is a restatement of the idea that people have good intentions and are able to respond—or not—based on what they learned during childhood. This is quite different from what Linda actually said earlier: "Part of her loved me beyond belief, and part of her wanted to destroy me"* [50:10].*) Is it or is it not? (*By posing an either/or question, Virginia makes it unlikely that Linda will qualify her answer.*)

53:26 LINDA: I'm kind of spacy, so could you say that again?

53:28 VIRGINIA: Yes. I'll put this (pillow) down now because we'll get this next time. Take both of my hands.

53:33 LINDA: OK.

53:34 VIRGINIA: What you said was, and it was brilliant what you said, in my opinion. (*Saying that what Linda said "was brilliant" gives Linda credit for the idea that Virginia introduced repeatedly earlier* [51:06].) You knew about your mother's heart. (*"You knew about . . . " presupposes that the mother's good heart did exist. It was to Linda's credit that she "knew" about it. The past tense— "knew"— gives mother's heart more reality by putting it with the memories from the past that Linda has been complaining about. Linda nods.*) She couldn't express what was in her heart, because, you said, of her upbringing. (*In Virginia's restatement of Linda's polarity, the part about her mother wanting to destroy Linda has been redescribed as an "inability to express what was in her heart," as a result of her mother's difficult upbringing.* [meaning reframing])

53:44   LINDA: Umhm.

53:45   VIRGINIA: Her upbringing is composed of all of these people.

53:48   LINDA: Umhm.

53:50   VIRGINIA: All right. Now, what I would like to do, from what you know, is I would like you—where is your grandmother and grandfather? (Linda indicates them with a gesture.) All right. Would you posture them in relation to each other, that shows where she was? Would you do that? Posture them. (*Virginia is beginning the process of creating a "family sculpture" or tableau that will show Linda what her mother experienced while she was growing up. Beginning with the grandparents, Linda will pose all the family members in relationship to each other, to create a family sculpture. Virginia begins to use this completed family sculpture with Linda at* [56:38].)

54:05   LINDA (to "grandmother"):   You need to be flat on the floor—

54:08   "LINDA'S GRANDMOTHER" (laughing):   Flat on the floor?

54:10   LINDA: —with a lot of ravioli around you. (laughter)

54:12   VIRGINIA: Flat on the floor. Well, could she just make it even more so, by putting her nose on the floor? (Linda demonstrates how her "grandmother" should hide her head in the crook of her elbow.) That's right, that's right. Good. That's the gesture you

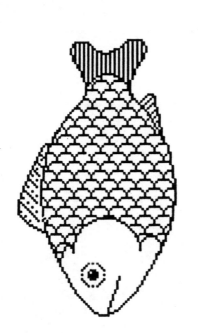

(Linda) used before, remember? [40:16] (*This is a nice example of Virginia's sensitivity to nonverbal gestures and the important messages they convey.*) Way down on the floor.

54:22   LINDA (demonstrating to "grandfather"):   You need to be like this, ready to kick her.

54:25   VIRGINIA: OK. (to Linda's heart) Now what I would like to do is to get down here just a little bit here (off a riser), down there, ready. (to "grandfather," who has put his hand on "grandmother's" head) No, you don't do that. It's too gentle. You're going to—while he's busy—that's right, the kicking part, OK? Now, while that's going on, who is the firstborn here?

54:38   LINDA (gesturing toward a woman):   Ah, this person.

54:41   VIRGINIA: All right, would you put that person, model that—posture that person in relation to this?

54:46   LINDA: Well, you need to be over next to him ("grandfather"), kind of like this. (Linda demonstrates a bowed head, hunched back, and hands together over the chest as if in prayer.)

54:52   VIRGINIA: Behind him, like he is her *shield*?

54:56   LINDA: No. No, you—he made you do lots of different things from a very young age—all highly intellectual things.

55:04   VIRGINIA: All right, so she's down there then—

55:06   LINDA: You're afraid of him.

55:08   VIRGINIA: She's down here on the floor, then, with him—

55:10   LINDA: Yeah.

55:11   VIRGINIA: —pleading and begging, down on the floor. (to first "sister") You go way down on the floor. Over a little bit in the front here, cowering in front of him. OK. Now the next one.

55:19   LINDA: My mother.

55:20   VIRGINIA: All right, so you now come in. You are the second, she's the first second born? (*Virginia often said, "Every child is the 'first' born: the first is the first first; the second is the first sec-*

ond . . . " to diffuse any evaluative connotation of "first" being "best.")

55:24   LINDA: Right.

55:25   VIRGINIA: Where do you put her?

55:27   LINDA: You need to be out over on this side, kind of in the same position that she [first "sister"] is, scrubbing the floor.

55:33   VIRGINIA: OK. Now with the next one.

55:35   LINDA: Boy, I'm not even sure. I think there was a brother.

55:38   VIRGINIA: Well?

55:39   LINDA: And I'm not sure of these people.

55:42   VIRGINIA: Does it really matter?

55:44   LINDA (to a "brother"):   OK, you just be hanging around looking really wimpy. (laughter)

55:48   VIRGINIA: What is he supposed to be doing?

55:49   LINDA: Hanging around looking wimpy.

55:51   VIRGINIA: Wimpy. All right, now when you say that, now what I understand is you mean this. (Virginia gestures toward the women already posed cowering on the floor.)

55:55   LINDA: Well, except that you are a man, so you are not quite cowering like this, but you just disappear sort of in the woodwork.

56:01   VIRGINIA: OK. All right. OK.

56:03   LINDA: And the other brothers do the same thing.

56:05   VIRGINIA: All right, just lower yourselves. And aren't they all in front of him, like he was the "big pasha" in this group?

56:11   LINDA: Right.

56:12   VIRGINIA: All right, so go in *front* so you look properly cowed. Heads bowed in front of your father. Now what about those two?

56:22 LINDA: You need to . . . also just be . . . staying as far away from him as possible, but not *too* far that he would be angry because you were *too* far away. And also looking sheepish and unobtrusive, both of you.

56:38 VIRGINIA (to the "family"): So you are full of shame, you are full of feeling victimized. You are full of fear, all of those words. (to Linda) Do they mean something to you? (*Virginia's question invites Linda to notice that the victimization her mother and siblings felt was similar to what Linda felt. She and her mother were really in the same position.*)

56:47 LINDA: I think so.

56:48 VIRGINIA: All right. (Virginia takes Linda's hand again.) *Shame* comes to me so *strongly* (Linda nods), and I hear, now *hear your mother say*, "What a *shame* it is that you don't do something with your music." (*By saying, "shame comes to me . . . and I hear, now hear your mother say . . . " Virginia begins by sharing her own experience, and—when she gets agreement from Linda—follows this with an embedded command for Linda to "hear your mother." Virginia then associates this entire scenario of shame, etc., with her mother's nagging Linda. This makes it even more explicit that the nagging that Linda experienced originates in her mother's past.* Linda nods.) Anyway, let's look at that now. (to the "family") Now I want you to make the sounds—everybody doing some kind of sound that fits your posture. Let's hear it. ("Grandfather" makes grunting sounds and hitting noises; everyone else groans or whimpers.)

57:14 VIRGINIA: Louder. (The sounds grow louder.)

57:16 VIRGINIA: Can you make some word sound that goes with that? [conversational postulate]

57:18 ALL: "I don't want to." "Don't!" "Please, no." "Please."

57:23 VIRGINIA: Louder. Louder. (The voices become louder.)

57:26 VIRGINIA: All right, let that fade. Let that fade. (to Linda) Tell me, what did you feel as you looked at that? (*Virginia has created this scenario for Linda in all major representational systems—visual, auditory, and kinesthetic feeling.*)

57:34   LINDA (voice breaking): Well, I felt really sad, and a lot of sympathy for my mother. My grandfather wasn't . . . angry enough, but that's OK.

57:46   VIRGINIA: OK. Yes, I could see that he wasn't. Now, Let's leave this for the moment. (to the "family") Don't get up, just stay right where you are. Now, how did he [Linda's "father"] get into this picture, to find her? (*Having set up the sculpture of the mother's childhood, Virginia will next bring Linda's father into the picture.*)

57:57   LINDA: He was . . . (Linda starts to cry) Um, he was funny. (*Linda is clearly feeling grief for the dead father she loved so much. It would be possible to pause here and deal with her grief, but Virginia continues to pursue Linda's original outcome.*)

58:10   VIRGINIA: Was funny? OK.

58:12   LINDA: And sang a lot.

58:14   VIRGINIA: OK. All right. (Linda cries.) So he hid his pain under being funny and sang—whatever else. (*Virginia presupposes that her father also had pain—he just hid it. This helps build a more balanced perception of mother and father as equals, instead of "devil and saint."*) But how did he get to know she was there? How did he even find out she was in the world?

58:28   LINDA (calmly):   Well, I believe people are drawn to each other. (*Linda doesn't answer Virginia's question. Even if people are drawn to each other, they have to meet somehow.*)

58:31   VIRGINIA: Well, how did he do it? Did—was he a friend of one of the brothers? Did he—did they go to a dance? How did he find out she was in the world?

58:39   LINDA: I really don't know on this level.

58:41   VIRGINIA: Make it up. (*This is an example of the "as–if" frame, or pretending. Virginia knows that whatever Linda "makes up" will have the same impact as if Linda remembered exactly what happened, because what she "makes up" will come out of her own mind, and it is in her mind that all this takes place. Most people's memories are inaccurate, partly or largely made up and fragmentary anyway, as Virginia alluded to earlier [46:01]. Linda quickly agrees to make it up.*)

58:43 LINDA: OK. They were at a party together, and they met at a party through mutual friends. And he was attracted to her because she was religious—a good Catholic—and very . . . had a lot of moral integrity.

59:02 VIRGINIA: All right, so he didn't expect her to "fool around"?

59:07 LINDA: Right.

59:08 VIRGINIA: He expected her to be an honest woman. Did that—

59:09 LINDA: And a good mother.

59:10 VIRGINIA: Did that mean that he came from a place where the woman was on the loose side? (*Virginia again tries to balance Linda's experience of her father's behavior as, like her mother's, coming out of past experiences.*)

59:14 LINDA: No he—his parents died when he was very young and he was the youngest, and the next sibling was twenty years older, so he was kind of alone.

59:24 VIRGINIA: So who took care of him?

59:26 LINDA: His older brother and his wife.

59:28 VIRGINIA: So, and there probably was—for him— nothing he could really put his hands to. (*Again Virginia directs Linda's attention to her father's experience resulting from his upbringing.*)

59:32 LINDA (agreeing):   No.

59:33 VIRGINIA: Was that wife loose? His brother's wife, was she on the loose side?

59:36 LINDA: I don't think so, I doubt it.

59:37 VIRGINIA: Well, somebody was loose in this family, I'll tell you that. (Linda laughs. *Virginia has seen so many families that she knows how often people search for opposite qualities in each other, to balance their own abilities or those of others in their families of origin. Virginia is helping Linda recognize this about her own parents, and also recognize that her father had his own weaknesses or limitations.*)

59:44   LINDA (emphatically, as if this is a sudden realization): *He was! He* was very loose, and very promiscuous and wild and crazy kind of guy.

59:46   VIRGINIA: OK. All right. OK. So now, he finds her. Now I would just like you for a moment to just think in terms of how people are. He's wild and loose, (Linda laughs) and she is very, very strong and looks like she is full of integrity. (*Virginia describes the father's behavior in terms that most people would not approve of—"wild and loose"—and describes the mother's behavior in terms that most would approve of—"strong, integrity." This will tend to balance Linda's earlier perception of her father as good and her mother as bad.*)

60:03   LINDA: Right.

60:04   VIRGINIA: Can you imagine that he would find that a support for him?

60:08   LINDA: Oh, definitely.

60:10   VIRGINIA: And that *she* would depend on him to bring light into her life?

60:13   LINDA (nodding):   Right.

60:14   VIRGINIA (to Linda's "father"):   All right, so what I would like you to do is sing in your best voice, and be as funny as you can, (Linda laughs) and go in there and *rescue her*. Just *rescue her*, and take her in your arms, just do that. Let's see it happen. Because that's what you do, because she is exactly right for you. So go in and do that.

60:30   LINDA (to Randy, her "father"):   You've got the right part! ("Father" looks up and hesitates.)

60:34   VIRGINIA: Let it happen. (*Virginia is presupposing that it will happen if he lets it.* Linda laughs.)

60:37   LINDA'S "FATHER":   Let me think a minute . . . . Um. (going over to Linda's mother) Why don't you come with me? We're going to go party tonight. There's a good party I know of. (He takes her hands and pulls her up.)

60:47   LINDA'S "MOTHER" (hesitant and a little frightened): Oh, oh.

60:48   LINDA'S "FATHER":   Do you want to come? Maria.

60:50   LINDA'S "MOTHER" (still hesitant):   I'd like to, um—

60:51   LINDA'S "FATHER":   Mar*ia*! (He starts singing the song of that name from the musical "West Side Story." The group laughs.)

60:54   VIRGINIA: Go ahead, that's lovely.

60:56   LINDA'S "FATHER" (singing):   I've just met a girl named Maria. (speaking) What's your real name?

60:59   LINDA'S "MOTHER":   Naomi.

61:00   LINDA'S "FATHER":   Naomi.

61:01   VIRGINIA (to "father" and "mother"):   All right, OK. Now, you can all fade for the moment, just fade a little bit. (to Linda) Now I want you to look at those two for the minute.

61:06   LINDA: OK.

61:07   VIRGINIA: And what do you feel now as you look at them?

61:10   LINDA (with expression):   They're cute! (Linda laughs.)

61:12   VIRGINIA: I'd like you to *keep that picture*, because that's exactly there. (*"I'd like you to keep that picture" is an embedded command to remember this scenario in order to maintain Linda's broadened representation of her parents.* Linda nods.) What he didn't know about her was that that rigidity would be over *everything*.

61:21   LINDA (nodding):   Umhm.

61:22   VIRGINIA: Way beyond her maturity—ah, her integrity. And his funniness would go against her feeling that there could be any order at all. And so he—what was used as a way to get together became a yoke around their necks. (*The complementary abilities that so often attract a couple to each other can also become sources of conflict and disagreement.*)

61:38   LINDA (nodding):   Umhm.

61:39   VIRGINIA: So by the time *you* came—now how many are in your—you had three? (*Now Virginia will add Linda's brothers and sisters—and finally Linda herself—to the family sculpture. Virginia's therapeutic work resumes at* [64:10].)

61:43   LINDA: And I'm the youngest.

61:45   VIRGINIA: You're the youngest. What were the two that came before you, brothers?

61:48   LINDA: A middle brother and older sister.

61:50   VIRGINIA: All right, would you find your older sister and your brother? (to "mother's family," joking) You can all just sit down now and thank God your life is over—*maybe.*

61:57   LINDA (gesturing to the last man in the group):   I have no choice.

61:59   VIRGINIA: Is this your older sister? (She points to a woman who has just stepped up.)

62:02   LINDA: Yes.

62:04   VIRGINIA: And where is your—?

62:05   LINDA: He's coming. No, he's leaving. No he's leaving.

62:07   VIRGINIA: All right.

62:08   LINDA: We've run out of men. Maybe I could pick a woman for my mother's heart, and he (gesturing toward the man who has been playing mother's heart) could be my brother right here.

62:12   VIRGINIA: All right, go ahead and do that.

62:14   LINDA: Would you be my brother now?

62:16   "MOTHER'S HEART":   OK. Whatever you like, Linda. (joking) I have such a big heart about this.

62:19   LINDA (to a woman):   Will you be my mother's heart?

62:21   VIRGINIA: And then what you do is to find—you have another sister?

62:25   LINDA: No.

62:26   VIRGINIA: Someone for you, someone—a stand-in for you.

62:30   LINDA: Somebody want to stand in for me? (Linda gestures toward a woman in the group.)

62:33   VIRGINIA: All right. Now I want you to posture these two, because I see what's happening here—they stopped doing that. (She is gesturing toward Linda's "parents," who are no longer embracing and enjoying each other.)

62:41   LINDA: Right.

62:42   VIRGINIA: All right. So what happened, then? Here's this firstborn child. My hunch is that your mother went like *this* (Virginia crosses "mother's" arms across her chest) after a while, and started moving off. (to "mother") Don't fall off of there [the riser she is standing on]. I don't want you to do that.

62:51   LINDA: Mother would be like this, but with her back turned (facing away from "father").

62:54   VIRGINIA: All right. OK. That's—

62:55   LINDA: And you (Linda's sister) would be over by my dad, holding his hand.

62:58   VIRGINIA: All right. All right. OK. And facing your mother's *back,* but probably not facing it at all—more facing your father. And now what about your brother? Where does he come?

63:10   LINDA: You are, um, off to the side of both of them, quite a ways, and you are shuffling your feet, and looking down at your feet.

63:20   VIRGINIA: OK.

63:23   "BROTHER":   Over here?

63:25   VIRGINIA: Yeah, but with your back to them. It's kind of "What are you doing in this world?" and I don't know what— "wimpy" is what you would say that behavior was, right?

63:30   LINDA: Oh, pretty angry, *sullen. Sullen* would be that.

63:33   VIRGINIA: Yeah, looks like a rain cloud. (to Linda) Now, for *you.* Put yourself in there. Where is she, where are you?

Your stand-in, here you are. (She gestures toward Linda's "stand-in.") Where are you?

63:47   LINDA: I am . . . um . . . skipping around on the outside as well. You don't have to skip, but I'm lightly—

63:57   VIRGINIA (to Linda's "stand-in"):   Yeah, you can skip around there. Just skip around and crawl over something, just be careful not to touch anybody too much. All right. And you be careful that you aren't all around here, either [near "mother" and "sister"]. (to Linda) OK. All right, when you look at that now, what do you feel? (*As Virginia describes Linda's stand-in's behavior—"just be careful you don't touch anybody too much," "be careful that you aren't all around here either" and " . . . when you look at that now"—Linda becomes a dissociated observer, watching this unhappy scene from the outside.*)

64:14   LINDA (almost crying, shaking her head):   *Sad.*

64:15   VIRGINIA: OK. (Virginia takes Linda's hand.) This wasn't always this way, but it was this way when you knew it. OK. Now, what happened to him? (Virginia gestures toward Linda's "brother.")

64:26   LINDA: He was . . . kind of beaten down by my father, because he wasn't coming through with what my father's dreams of himself were. And he was . . . really (shaking her head) distorted by my mother.

64:45   VIRGINIA: All right, now what you are talking about, if I were to meet him today, one of the things that I would see is that he would be very shy and not want to put himself forward. (*Virginia translates Linda's description of her brother's past into his likely behavior in the present, again linking the past to present behavior.*)

64:54   LINDA: He's an alcoholic, and he's very withdrawn.

64:56   VIRGINIA: Yeah, and so then he would have to do something like that. So that you're alcoholic today. That doesn't mean that you aren't bright or nice. It means that when the pain comes, you drown it. And what happened to your sister, your older sister?

65:10 LINDA: She . . . ran away . . . and then became a mother . . . and then ran away from that and became a hippie. And now she's "born again."

65:20 VIRGINIA: OK. So what she did (to the "sister"), so we just see you running out, and then you run back, then you run out again, and run back. So, if you don't mind doing that, you can do that. And you?

65:30 LINDA: You . . . um . . . (Linda's voice starts to break.)

65:35 VIRGINIA: That's "me" you're talking about.

65:37 LINDA: Right. You . . . hung in there . . . (crying) and tried to make everybody happy.

65:45 VIRGINIA: OK. Did you succeed, even a little bit?

65:49 LINDA: Oh, yeah (nodding).

65:50 VIRGINIA (softly):   I want you to be in touch with that. OK. What are you feeling right now as you are letting yourself know that?

66:02 LINDA: Um . . . it's a *burden.*

66:07 VIRGINIA: OK. Now what I would like to have—show you. I want all of you to take your postures real tight, real tight. Everybody, to take your postures that you got *real tight.* (to Linda's self-worth) And you know about that tightness, that's why you cry. You are the self-worth, right? (*Seeing this, and feeling the uncomfortable tightness so strongly, gives Linda motivation—something to move away from.*)

66:27 VIRGINIA: Here's mother's heart which beats. And I want you to be like a metronome, beating, just beating: um um um um, back and forth. (*Mother's heart is something positive Linda can move toward.*)

66:36 VIRGINIA: And I want you [Linda's self-worth] to cry a little bit, and that represents the cry from all over here (gesturing toward the family sculpture). Now, I'm going to ask all of you now to let yourself . . . give yourself a message of appreciation and start it off by taking a breath, let your body fill with air, and as you do, let your body expand to meet the air that comes into you until your whole

body is standing upright, and you are free to move in any way you can
... Let that all happen. Letting ... and testing your moving, back and
forth. Now when you get on your own feet, look around, and as you
see people, do what you want to do with them ... and do it. (People
start hugging each other. *The foregoing is essentially a hypnotic induction, with everything presupposed by "let yourself," which indicates
that all that Virginia said will occur unless people don't "let it happen." Virginia has moved through a sequence from tightness to appreciation and breathing, to standing upright, to physical movement, to
contacting people actively. The contrast created between the unde-
sirable tension and the liberating "expansion" makes the desirability
of the solution even stronger.*)

67:40   VIRGINIA: Now, what I want to find out from you,
Linda—what did you see here?

67:44   LINDA: (softly and tearfully) It was transformed into
love.

67:47   VIRGINIA: Yes. And you know how it happened?

67:54   LINDA (shaking her head): No.

67:55   VIRGINIA: What did I say? I'm going to act like a
schoolteacher for a minute. What did I do? What directions did I give
to make this change?

68:07   LINDA: You asked them to breathe.

68:09   VIRGINIA: Yes. And then?

68:11   LINDA: I'm not sure I was listening.

68:13   VIRGINIA: OK. I'm glad you are telling me that,
(*Virginia responds to Linda's not listening in a positive way. Rather
than treating it as a problem, she says, "I'm glad you are telling me
that."*) because it's very important. When I asked them to breathe,
then I asked them to let their bodies expand to meet the breath that
was going on. Now do you remember that you heard it? (*Virginia
gestures toward Linda, presupposing that Linda heard it; it's only a
question of whether she remembers it now.*)

68:27   LINDA: Vaguely.

68:29   VIRGINIA: OK. And that's all right, because you were involved with other things. (*Virginia again acknowledges Linda's not remembering or hearing in a positive way.*) And then I said, "Now what fits for you, standing on your own feet?" And did you notice what they did? What did you see them do?

68:40   LINDA: They stood up and . . . looked alive and . . . (almost crying) nurtured people.

68:47   VIRGINIA: All right. Now you see this lady ("mother") right here. This is a lady that behaved in relation to (gesturing toward "mother's" family)—not this [embracing], because she didn't know about that—in relation to the best that she knew how, which is [to] try to get her kids to do it. And she wasn't all that successful, but she tried hard. (*Virginia reiterates the reframe that Linda's mother's intentions were good, and that she did the best she could, within her limited world.*) Now, as you look at her from here, what are you aware of feeling toward her?

69:10   LINDA (softly):   I feel a lot more compassion.

69:12   VIRGINIA (speaking in a hypnotic tone of voice):   Can you move a little closer to her, and see what that feels like? [conversational postulate] (Linda walks over to her "mother" and they embrace warmly for some time.) As close as you want to feel, OK. And let yourself be in touch as you are here now, being aware that what you are *now* touching is the life force of your mother. [presupposition] What you saw *before* were the behaviors that came out because the life force didn't have a place to express itself, and that's a self-worth view. (*Again Virginia makes the distinction between Linda's old perceptions of her mother's behaviors and the mother's internal life—good intentions and nurturing.*) What do you feel, self-worth?

69:40   "SELF-WORTH":   Ummm! I'm feeling, really . . . a tremendous amount of love and . . . ah . . . overwhelming.

69:49   VIRGINIA: Now when you come to your owner [embedded command], you don't have to cry anymore. (*Virginia connects Linda's being in touch with her mother's "life force" and positive intentions with Linda gaining her own positive self-worth.*)

69:52   "SELF-WORTH":   Umhm.

69:53   VIRGINIA: Do you want to come over? (Linda's "self-worth" goes to Linda and they embrace.) And you can enjoy her, and she can enjoy you, but it's *life* that she's enjoying. (Virginia speaks to Linda.) How was that for you? How was that for you?

70:04   LINDA: It was . . . I don't know. I don't know if I can put it in words. It was very helpful, very . . . graphic . . . . It's . . . it's ah—it's something that I would desperately love to be able to translate into my life, what I'm feeling now. And have been missing the plug—the connection. I just—I—how do I then talk to my mother differently? (*Linda is presupposing that she will talk to her mother differently, yet she has some doubt as to exactly how she will do this.*)

70:35   VIRGINIA: Can you see yourself doing whatever the "it" is? [conversational postulate] (*This is a direct instruction to Linda to see herself communicating with her mother differently in the future.*)

70:39   LINDA (looks up to her right briefly, and then answers confidently):   Yes, I can. (Linda nods and smiles.)

70:41   VIRGINIA: OK. All right, because your eyes have changed. (Linda nods.) There's a different expression in your eyes (Linda nods), and there's a different expression in your face right here (gesturing toward Linda's cheeks). And that says to me that you have *moved* into another place in yourself. (Linda nods. *Virginia knows that Linda has reached her outcome by the nonverbal shifts visible in her eyes and cheeks. She didn't need a followup study to find out if she was successful.*) And I don't *know* what the exact words will be (gesturing toward Linda's "mother"). I don't *know* what the transactions will be (gesturing toward Linda's "mother"), but one thing I *do* know is that you will never look at your mother again in the same way. (Virginia gestures from Linda to her "mother." Linda nods.) And *she* will never look at you in the same way (gesturing from Linda's "mother" to Linda), because you will come in with something different. (*Virginia is saying that since Linda's perceptions are changed, she will act differently with her mother; this change in Linda's behavior will cause her mother to perceive Linda differently and to respond and act differently toward Linda.* Linda nods.) And now all the stuff about having to yell at her and so on is really irrelevant. (Virginia gestures to Linda's right. Linda nods.)

(The preceding is a straightforward "post-hypnotic induction" or "future-pace" loaded with presuppositions that connect what Linda has learned in this session with Virginia to where she needs it—in future interactions with her mother. Virginia begins by describing the changes in Linda's face, which indicate Linda has changed, using present tense to reinforce the change. She then shifts to "have moved into another place . . . "the present perfect tense that indicates a completed past. Then she speaks of her own knowing in the present that Linda will be different in the future. "You will never look at your mother again in the same way" describes and ratifies the shift Linda has made as permanent and lasting. Then Virginia returns to present tense, describing Linda's former need to yell as irrelevant, and setting it off to the side with a gesture. [temporal predicate shifts])

71:18   VIRGINIA (turning toward the group):   Are you aware of that? We went through a period where what we were doing is castigating everybody. That was supposed to be for health—telling how bad our parents were, and all the rest of it. That's not where it is at all.

(In a six-minute segment that is omitted from the videotape because it isn't directly relevant to Virginia's work with Linda, Virginia asks all the participants to share how they are feeling, if they wish, just as she did with Linda's self-worth earlier [69:38]. *She does this both to include group members in the process, and to check for any unresolved unpleasant feelings about the roles they played, etc. After checking with all the other participants, Virginia again turns to Linda.)*

71:28   VIRGINIA: And now, how about you, love?

71:31   LINDA: Twenty words or less? (The group laughs.)

71:34   VIRGINIA (softly):   Whatever you want to say, love. I know that a lot of things can't go into words. All I'm asking is if you have any, would you like to share them? *(Virginia acknowledges that a lot has happened nonverbally, even if Linda doesn't have words to express it.)*

71:43   LINDA: I feel (looking to her left, searching for words) something has shifted . . . and I think you're right that I won't ever be able to look at my mother in the same way again. *(Linda's choice of words indicates that the shift in her perception is now automatic—*

even if she tries, she "won't be able to" see her mother in the same way again.) Um . . . (looking to her left and also down left) I feel clearer, and much more loving. I'm in love with everyone in the room. (Linda smiles.)

72:04   VIRGINIA: Wonderful. Wonderful, wonderful. [repetition] (Virginia and Linda embrace.)

72:09   LINDA (with her hands still on Virginia's shoulders): Thank you very much for doing that. (Linda gazes directly into Virginia's eyes.) That was wonderful for me.

72:12   VIRGINIA: This—you did a universal trip. (Linda nods.) There are very few people in the world who couldn't have taken this trip with you. Maybe not in the same—feeling the same way with mother— (Linda nods, and Virginia turns to face the group, and speaks in a humorously outraged tone of voice.) But how many of us feel that our growing up was deficient? Heavens! We should have been born to the most *exciting, intelligent, right* people all the time. What was the matter with them that they got their egg and sperm together and activated us when they weren't *really there* to do it? Huh? (*Bringing this back to the universal level invites the audience— and all of us—to find similar opportunities to apply this knowledge in our own lives. In addition to making the session more useful to the audience, this again treats Linda as equal to the rest of us.*) Wonderful, OK. Thank you very much. (All on stage with Virginia return to their seats.)

72:50   VIRGINIA: I have spoken to you about the fact that I have been working with families for over forty years, and I see a lot of things. Everything that I strive for, you just saw.

Followup Interview

In August 1989, almost three and a half years after her session with Virginia, Linda met with Connirae Andreas to record how Linda's experience with Virginia had affected her life and her relationship with her mother. This interview is also included in the videotape "Forgiving Parents" (1989).

72:55 CONNIRAE: Linda, now that it is about three years since your session with Virginia, we're interested to find out what your perspective is now on the impact that that's had on your experience.

73:04 LINDA: Hm. Well, it was interesting. It's been something that I haven't been able to forget, and have talked about with friends—in fact, have laughed about with friends, especially some of the friends that were there in the audience with me, or people who have *become* friends. And, you know, the person that was my *heart* in that tape, and the person that was my mother in that tape or my father, where—we actually wound up having discussions about that episode, and being that vulnerable and . . . it's affected, I think, my relationship with my mother, and it's also affected my work, and even when I notice the way parents talk to their children, and I am aware of how wonderful the gems were that she had.

73:58 CONNIRAE: So it sounds like it's had a fairly broad impact in a lot of areas.

74:02 LINDA: Oh, I'll never forget it.

74:04 CONNIRAE: And if we could go into some of the areas—how has it been different with your mother? What's happened there?

74:12 LINDA: Well, I think that I did a lot of thinking after that session happened, because I spent, what, an hour or an hour and a half having to—in front of what I felt at the time was the world— talk about my mother and my relationship, and I felt real upset and tearful and I came away, I think, with a whole lot more compassion about my mother and what she's been through in her life, and it's changed my position on how I look at her, and how I feel about her.

74:48 CONNIRAE: So, do you do things differently with her now than you would have before?

74:51 LINDA: Oh, yeah. I look at her differently. I've had occasions—lots of occasions—where I've been sitting across the table from my mom, and nobody else was in the house, and I will ask her things about her life. "How did her parents treat her?" And in fact she said to me, "Well, I think that my father would have been arrested for child abuse today if he had done things today to me that he did fifty [years ago]." My mother is old enough to be my grandmother, so we really skipped a generation. She had me when she was forty-four. So there was a big generation gap there.

75:33   LINDA: And I have gotten a lot of insights into how she was raised, and why she was so critical of me because of some of the things that happened to her. And she opened her heart to me in lots of ways. In fact, I felt like I was her best friend, which was *really* something I would never ever have said before. But having listened to Virginia and watched her work with some of the other people that were there, I pulled some of those techniques and just incorporated them in my relationship with my mother. I spent more time after that asking my mother questions. Um, if we were taking a trip together—and I tried to invite her to go on day trips. If I had to go up into the mountains for my work, I would ask her if she wanted to come along, and in those car trips I asked her about her life.

76:23   LINDA: "What was your dad like to you? And if you wanted—if you chose to have kids all over again, would you do that?' And I really tried to listen to the answers that she gave, and I started recognizing—this sounds kind of weird but I said to myself, "Boy, Linda, if you think *you* had it bad having her as a mother, imagine what it was like for her having *them* as her parents,' because she had some tough parents. She had, you know, Italian immigrant parents who were very hard on her. So I just started personalizing, I guess, my relationship with her more.

77:00   CONNIRAE: Great. So it sounds like that's been a lot more positive for you.

77:04   LINDA: Yes. Oh, it has. Definitely.

77:06   CONNIRAE: Probably for her, too.

77:08   LINDA: I would think so, although I don't get that feedback from her, because she's not a person that shares that kind of stuff, but I definitely think just because she did open up to me, that she feels that way, too. But I had to make the change, you see. It wasn't—for a long time I think I waited for my mother to change. "Why does she do this, and why does she do that?" And what—one of the things that came out of working with Virginia was, it's *my* work, and *I'm* the one that needs to shift my position, or try something else.

77:37   CONNIRAE: Well, that's a big shift.

77:39   LINDA: Yeah, it is.

77:40   CONNIRAE: Good, and you mentioned also that it had an impact on some other areas of your life. Can you say a little bit more about that—if it shifted your way of being in some other areas, too?

77:52   LINDA: My work is as a teacher. I have my own consulting business, and teach workshops to adults and parents and community members and most recently, in the past couple of years, I've shifted to youth leadership trainings where I will work with teenagers, high school kids, who will talk to me about their parents. And high school kids typically are complaining about their parents. And they are talking about how their parents don't listen to them, or they are never validated, or all their parents do is pick on the things that they don't do well, and not say to them how much they care about them, or why they appreciate them being in their lives. And I've seen myself do some Virginia Satir tricks where I will say to them, "You know, you might be the one that needs to tell your mom first that you are glad that she's your mom. If you are waiting for your mom to tell you, she may not be the one to do that. You may have to say, "You know, Mom, I know you really do sacrifice a lot for us and I really appreciate it," and that kind of stuff.

78:44   CONNIRAE: So you are passing on your learnings to others, too. Great. Thinking back on it now, are there any other comments that you have about your experience there?

78:57   LINDA: I can't get the—the image that sticks out in my mind the most—other than seeing this imposing, powerful woman next to me in her flowered dress—was the image I have of her working with the mother and the little child (later in the workshop), bringing the little child up on a chair so that the two were looking eye to eye. And I don't know why that was so profound for me, but it symbolized to me how important it is to really look eye to eye. I mean, with my own internal little girl, in that process as well as—maybe it's the old Indian saying of "walk a mile in the other person's moccasins" that was profound to me. And the whole experience of being *that* open, and pouring out that part of me, was something I'll never forget.

79:51   LINDA: *And* the way that she treated people is a message that I just take wherever I go. That respect and dignity that she tried to create between people. In my work with teenagers, they are perceived as powerless. The adults have all the power. And my work a lot is having teams of young people and adults come together to work in partnership. And the adults usually take over, and the teenagers are always trying to get a word in edgewise. And using some of those Virginia Satir things to have people be more on an equal basis is another thing I've taken from that experience.

80:31   CONNIRAE: Great. That sounds good, too. Well, I want to thank you for coming back and letting us know that impact for you. And I'm guessing some of those similar impacts will be going [to happen] with a lot of the people who view this tape. Oh, I am curious about whether you were surprised to actually work with Virginia that much on stage, or if that was something that you like to do a lot in workshops.

80:57   LINDA: Well, I was shocked. I only thought I was going to be a member of the studio audience. That was the agreement. "Would you come and just take up some space in the audience and clap?" And I raised my hand to make some kind of a comment, and before I knew it she was saying, "Come on up here. Come on up here on stage." And literally, I don't remember the beginning of that session. I do not remember how it started, or how I was swept into it. I'm kind of curious to see, after three years, what happened. Because I don't remember. People were *so* unbelievable to me after that. People were coming up to me again and again saying, "Thank you so much for sharing that. I saw my mom," or, "I saw my relationship with my dad," or—and I realized that that "speaking the truth" stuff is real powerful. Not just the good stuff, but the dark or heavy stuff, or hard stuff.

81:50   CONNIRAE: I think a lot of other people will have the opportunity to do that through the videotape. Well, thank you again.

81:57   LINDA: You're welcome. Thank you.

Summary

No summary can do justice to the complexity and detail of Virginia's session with Linda. Yet no matter how limited it is, a summary is useful if it helps organize and direct our activities. The perceptions and beliefs that we all use to guide our actions are also brief summaries of our experiences. And like any other summary, these perceptions and beliefs are often limited, distorted, and over-generalized in ways that lead to unhappiness.

One way to think about this session is to see that Virginia worked systematically to broaden and enrich Linda's perceptions. This additional information then provided a basis for changing Linda's conclusions, beliefs, and feelings about her mother, herself, and her situation. These new perceptions and beliefs in turn established a firm foundation for more positive behavior.

One essential distinction that Virginia makes repeatedly is between Linda's actual mother and the image that Linda carries with her. Virginia realizes that Linda needs to come to terms with this image within herself. This is first brought up at 8:03, and later at 11:25, 15:48, 16:00, 32:46, 33:44, 43:02, 43:57, and 45:48.

The distinction between our image of the world and what's "actually out there" opens an empowering pathway to change. Knowing that all we have are images of the world makes us realize that whatever image we have is likely to be inaccurate and distorted in some way. At the same time, since images can be changed much more

easily than the world, this knowledge also provides us with the freedom and ability to see things differently. When we realize that conflicts result from images within ourselves, then we can take on the
responsibility for change gladly, rather than feeling that we are helpless victims, demanding that others change, and blaming or attacking
them when they don't.

By asking Linda about her mother's experiences before Linda
was born, Virginia enriched Linda's perspective. Virginia first speaks
to Linda about her mother's critical behavior having resulted from
her difficult upbringing at 25:45. She repeats this theme at 27:00,
27:38, 29:51, 30:50, and 37:08. Virginia introduces the same idea
with respect to Linda's own behavior at 35:36 and again at 53:10 and
68:47.

Initially Linda saw her problems with her mother *only* from her
own point of view. During the session Virginia repeatedly has Linda
consider, and then "become," aspects of her mother's experience, particularly her history, feelings, yearnings, and intentions. After the session Linda can also see the situation from her mother's point of view.
"Boy, Linda, if you think *you* had it bad having her as a mother, imagine what it was like for her having *them* as parents, because she had
some tough parents" [76:50]. In the followup interview Linda also
says, "It's the old Indian saying of 'walk a mile in the other person's
moccasins' that was profound to me" [79:40].

At the beginning of the session, Linda is only aware of her
mother's behavior and her own feelings of being a helpless victim in
response to it. At the end of the session she is also aware of her
mother's perceptions, thoughts, and feelings, and she understands
how her mother's past and Linda's own behavior affect her mother.

Virginia used these expanded perceptions to change Linda's
beliefs. Early in the session Linda believes that her mother had evil
intentions, and that her critical behavior was evidence that her mother
hated Linda. When Virginia states this for her—"She was trying to
make your life miserable" [15:57]—Linda agrees emphatically—
"*Absolutely!*" In contrast, at the end of the session Linda sees that
her mother had good intentions—"She loved me beyond belief"—and
that her mother's critical, hurtful behavior was simply a result of her
mother being limited by her own difficult experiences while growing
up.

This additional information provided a basis for Linda to reconsider her beliefs about her mother, and to acccpt the alternative presuppositions that Virginia offered. At the beginning of the session, Linda blamed her mother; now, if she has to blame somebody, she can blame her mother's family background.

Of course, the same insight can be applied to previous generations, so really there is no blame anywhere. If Linda were still in contact with her grandparents, it would be important to do this explicitly so that she wouldn't start blaming them instead of her mother.

At the beginning of the session Linda thought her mother should change. In the followup interview, Linda recognized that she could take the initiative to change the relationship. "I had to make the change, you see" [77:20]. "It's my work, and I'm the one that needs to shift my position, or try something else" [77:36]. Virginia first offers Linda this idea at 27:38 and again at 31:38, 37:26, 37:37, and 37:53. Linda mentions in the followup interview how she also carried this view into her own work with adolescents who want their parents to change, offering them the same empowering idea [78:35].

With these key perceptions and understandings—as well as all the others noted in the transcript—Linda can see herself and her mother as equals, each doing her best in life with what they know and can do. In the followup interview, the image that "sticks out" in Linda's mind is of Virginia later in the workshop, "working with the mother and the little child, bringing the little child up on a chair so that the two were looking eye to eye. And I don't know why that was so profound for me, but it symbolized to me how important it is to really look eye to eye" [79:10]. Linda also mentions "that respect and dignity that she [Virginia] tried to create between people" [79:57].

Working with such fundamental and universal ideas generates more extensive personal change than working with a particular "problem situation," because these new presuppositions will become influential throughout Linda's life. Presuppositions are not usually changed with a single utterance; it typically takes repetition to create a compelling personal experience of the truth and usefulness of thinking about things in a new way. There are a number of ways to create this kind of compelling personal experience; Virginia did it primarily by providing a living example, and through the experiences that roleplays provided. As the transcript shows, Virginia worked patiently and systematically to change Linda's thinking and understanding in order to reach the resolution that Linda wanted.

Virginia always moved from the specific complaints that clients brought her to larger and more universal issues. This is why we can all identify so easily with Linda on her journey and learn personally relevant lessons from it. All of us can think of people we criticize, blame, or hate because we don't yet understand that they, too, are doing the best they can—limited by their backgrounds, misconceptions, and confusions.

The positive presuppositions discussed here and in the transcript are powerful, but they are seldom conveyed by words alone. Virginia's modeling of these presuppositions in her own behavior—both verbal and nonverbal—was essential. She didn't just think that these empowering presuppositions were useful ways to induce change. She conveyed by her every word and gesture that she completely believed that people had good intentions, could learn anything, and could redirect their lives. Virginia's congruent, living example of these presuppositions made them easier to absorb for those she worked with, because she provided a nonverbal demonstration of doing what she was talking about.

Virginia Satir thus offered us a dual gift. She demonstrated the empowering beliefs she helped others adopt, and she offered precision in her behavior and change language that made it easy for others to respond to what she demonstrated. Although Virginia is gone, her message of hope and possibility lives on in those she touched, and in the work of those who are willing to make the effort to learn how to do what she did so beautifully.

Human contact is not about words. Human contact is about eye connection, about voice, about skin, about breathing. Words are something you can read in a book, you can see on a billboard, and they can be totally differentiated from human beings. Words help when people are congruent.

—VIRGINIA SATIR (1989)

Appendix I
Presuppositions

One of the most powerful patterns in the transcript of Virginia Satir's work with Linda is her use of presuppositions to change Linda's perceptions and beliefs. The power of presuppositions to bring about therapeutic change is vastly underappreciated, even by those with good hypnotic training. People can agree or disagree with direct statements, but presuppositions are typically accepted unconsciously and not even noticed consciously. Some examples of other master therapists' use of presuppositions illustrate this well.

Carl Whitaker

About eight years ago I observed Whitaker interview a couple on the first day of a weekend workshop. The couple had been divorced for five years, and had been in therapy longer than that. They sat next to each other in excellent nonverbal rapport, matching each other's body posture and breathing.

During the interview, they were reasonable and considerate with each other. Clearly, they had worked through their differences over the years. I found myself wondering why they didn't remarry; they seemed to get along so well.

Since there wasn't much for Whitaker to do with the couple, he asked them to bring in their two teenage sons the next day. The "rebel" son who lived with the father did not come in, but the "model" son who lived with the mother did.

The contrast with the previous day was striking. The mother and father sat much farther apart, with the son between them and much closer to the mother. Although the father's behavior was about the same as on the previous day, the mother was transformed. She was far more animated and sexy, particularly when talking to, or about, her son—which was most of the time. She spoke at length about how many activities they shared, how she confided in him, how well they got along together, etc. Whether you call this "enmeshment" or "violation of generational boundaries," it was clear that the mother was overinvolved with her son, and was responding to him much more like a lover than a son.

Right after the mother had related yet another example of how well she and her son got along, Whitaker gestured to her and to her son as he said, "So your second marriage worked out much better than your first one," and then gestured toward the father. The mother looked as if her brain had stopped working for several seconds. Obviously she had never thought of her relationship with her son as a "marriage" before; from then on it would be impossible for her to keep from thinking of it in that way. As Whitaker is fond of saying, "People can agree with me, or they can disagree with me, *but they can't ignore me.*"

Much of the power of Whitaker's statement to the mother comes from his *presupposing* that they are married. She can agree that her second marriage is better, or disagree and say that it isn't better, but it is much harder for her to reject the presupposition that she is acting as if she is married to her son—particularly when she has just completed a long list of interactions that are typical of a good marriage!

Even if the mother consciously rejects Whitaker's remark, it will still have its impact. Since most parents don't want to be married to their children, the mother can't avoid considering her involvement with her son in this light. Before, she had only been thinking, "Do I have a close relationship with my son or not?" Now, she will think, "Is it too close? Am I treating him like a spouse?" and she will avoid acting in ways that are too intimate. The son will do the same with his mother.

Milton Erickson

In the late 1950s, Milton Erickson was a guest speaker demonstrating his work at the VA Hospital in Palo Alto, California. Psychiatrists brought in their toughest clients for Erickson to work with one at a time.

One of these clients was a young man who had committed a wide variety of serious violent offenses. He had been waiting in the hall, watching as other patients were taken in and brought out later—often still clearly in trance.

When they finally took the young man in, he had no idea what awaited him. Erickson first asked the psychiatrist, "Why have you brought this boy to me?" After the psychiatrist listed the many offenses the boy had committed, Erickson commanded the psychiatrist, "Go sit down." Erickson then turned to the boy, gazed intently into his eyes, and said, "How surprised will you be when all your behavior changes completely next week?" The boy looked startled and said, "I'll be *very* surprised!" Erickson then turned to the psychiatrist and said, "Take this boy away." The psychiatrist thought that Erickson had decided not to work with him. However, a week later all the boy's destructive behavior did, in fact, change completely.

Erickson had undoubtedly noticed the boy's heightened receptivity, and decided to deliver the presupposition that all his behavior would change. Erickson didn't ask the boy, "Will your behavior change or not?" Erickson's question *presupposed* that the boy's behavior would change; it's only a question of how *surprised* the boy will be *when* it changes.

When the boy's response—verbal and nonverbal—told Erickson that the boy had completely accepted this presupposition, he knew he had succeeded, so he dismissed him to avoid undoing what he had accomplished. If the boy had said, "I *would* be surprised," or if he had looked doubtful, Erickson would have gone on to try some other intervention. However, the boy said, "I *will be* very surprised," indicating that he had accepted Erickson's presupposition that the change would occur.

There were other important presuppositions that supported this brilliant intervention. When Erickson asks, "Why have you brought this *boy* to me?" he presupposes that the patient is a child, with all that that connotes—being immature, having a lot to learn, being dependent, needing guidance, etc. Then when he commands the psychiatrist to "Go sit down," Erickson presupposes that the psychiatrist (who has been in a parental role to the "boy" he brought) is himself in a position to take orders from Erickson.

With these two short utterances, Erickson sets himself up as an authority superior to those who have been dealing with the boy—all by presupposition and implication. Without these earlier presuppositions, it is unlikely that his later question would have had such impact.

Most of the presuppositions that are useful in therapy are not as global as this example of Erickson's, or as stunning as the Whitaker example. Nevertheless, they can be just as effective in getting significant shifts in perception and behavior. A number of small presuppositional shifts can work together to affect families powerfully.

Salvador Minuchin

One of my favorite examples of the use of successive presuppositions is a session in which Minuchin is seeing a family for the first time.

The problem that brings the family in is that the ten-year-old son is sniffing gasoline. Immediately after the introductions, Minuchin turns to the boy and says, "I understand you like to sniff gasoline. What do you think you are, an automobile?" This joking comment had an immediate impact. Everyone relaxed a little, and the problem became a little less insoluble.

The joke is fairly obvious. Not so obvious is the presupposition that serious matters can be discussed with humor. Even less apparent is the fact that Minuchin has planted a presupposition by using the words "you like to." In contrast, "You sniff," or "You have to," or "You feel driven to" would deliver very different presuppositions about the problem. Those kinds of statements would presuppose that the behavior is out of the boy's control, and therefore difficult to change. "You like to" presupposes that the behavior results from the child's own *desires,* not some crazy or incomprehensible compulsion.

In his next statement to the boy, Minuchin builds on this: "Which do you prefer—unleaded or regular?" Everyone relaxes a bit more as this second joking comment shifts the family's attention again. They were thinking of the boy's behavior as a serious problem beyond everyone's control, not as an expression of the child's preferences. Of course, the consequences of sniffing gasoline can be serious. Nevertheless, refocusing the family's attention in this way makes the problem easier to solve.

Next Minuchin smells and then takes a sip of the herb tea he has been holding, and says, "I wonder what kind of tea this is." Then he turns to the boy, offers him his cup, and says, "Since you have a good nose, tell me what kind of tea this is." This comment builds on the previous ones, refocusing attention from preference to the learned ability that makes preference possible. Minuchin has also presupposed that the boy "has a good nose," and is able to make some discriminations that Minuchin can't. This makes the boy superior to Minuchin in this respect, and alters the implicit hierarchy of the superior therapist/needy family.

When the family came in, they probably thought of the boy's behavior as crazy, incomprehensible, and uncontrollable. With three short comments Minuchin has transformed the family's perceptions. Now they are thinking of the behavior as an expression of the boy's preferences, and one that demonstrates a positive ability to discriminate. The "uncontrollable problem" is already three significant steps closer to a solution, because family members are thinking about it in a very different way. Rather than criticizing, reprimanding, or interrogating the boy, Minuchin has implicitly complimented him on his skill at discrimination. This provides a positive basis for guiding the boy toward using these skills in ways other than sniffing gasoline.

Of course, more needed to be done. Minuchin gathered information that demonstrated that the boy was a "parental child" with major responsibility for his four-year-old twin brothers, and he worked toward reorganizing the family so that the ten-year-old could have his own childhood, free of parental responsibilities.

Training in Presuppositions

Although these (and other) master therapists have demonstrated how to use presuppositions with powerful effect, very few therapy training programs systematically teach trainees how to construct them, or how to use nonverbal behavior to deliver them for full impact.

Fewer still teach how to detect and use subtle nonverbal cues to know whether the presuppositions have been accepted or not.

There seems to be a widespread prejudice in therapy against any training that divides global generalizations like "human contact," "intimacy," "self-worth," "triangulation," "codependence," "enmeshment," etc., into their constituent perceptions, feeling responses, and behaviors.

Few people would say that a love of music will by itself produce a great pianist without considerable practice at scales, timing, different styles of music, etc. Yet often the same people will tell you that all you need to do great therapy is to be caring and sensitive.

Although language is one of the principal tools of a therapist, most therapists know no more about how to use language than the people who come to see them. Family therapy has had many notable successes; the evolution of the field will require fewer global generalizations and more precision.

For an example, let's return to presuppositions. After studying the work of Virginia Satir and Milton Erickson, Bandler and Grinder (1975a) delineated twenty-nine linguistically distinct kinds of presuppositions. The five categories of simple presuppositions are somewhat trivial and not particularly useful. However, the twenty-four complex categories are very useful. Since different clients respond more fully to certain kinds of presuppositions than to others, it's useful for a therapist to be able to generate every kind of presupposition at will. Since each kind of presupposition is clearly specified, if they are practiced one at a time, they can quickly become an automatic part of a therapist's verbal behavior. Without this kind of practice, most therapists use only a few presuppositions, and sometimes even use these in ways that *impede* reaching the goal, rather than in ways that support it.

After learning how to generate each kind of presupposition, the next step is to start with a specific outcome, such as to get a father to touch his child lovingly, and to practice constructing different kinds of presuppositions to elicit that response. "*As you touch your child lovingly* next week, I'd like you to pay particular attention to—"; "If you are looking carefully at your child *when you touch him—*"; "Do you think anything could stop you from carrying out your *wish to touch him* more often?"; "Do you think *your touching your child* more will

actually allow you to notice your feelings of caring more fully?";
"I'm wondering whether the second or third time *you find yourself
touching your child caringly* will seem different from the first time.";
"How will your wife respond as she sees *you touching Billy gently?*";
"Who do you think *already enjoys touching him the most?*"; etc. This
kind of question can have tremendous impact, because in order to
answer, the *father has to imagine the experience of touching his child.*
In contrast, the father's experience would be very different if we asked,
"What has made you so cold and distant with your son?"

After some practice generating presuppositions, it also becomes
easier to recognize them in your own and the client's utterances. In an
exercise trainees can be asked to write down their typical opening
sentence to a client and then examine it for presuppositions. We suggest that you pause to write down your own typical beginning sentence to clients before reading further.

Many therapists start by asking, "How can I help you?" This
presupposes "I can help you," a complimentary "helper-helpee" relationship. This is a "welcome mat" for future dependence and "passive" behavior.

By contrast, "What changes do you want to achieve today?"
presupposes that rapid changes—plural—are possible, and also presupposes that the client is in the active role: The *client* is the one who
both *wants* and *achieves* changes, not the therapist.

"What is the problem?" directs the client to the past, in a search
for what didn't work. This is an invitation to endless "archaeology," a
return to what Virginia Satir called "the museum."

In contrast, "What kind of a relationship do you want to have
with your husband?" directs the client to think of desired outcomes.
From there it is a shorter step to develop specific ways to reach those
outcomes and leave the problem behind.

It is amazing how powerfully the presuppositions in the therapist's first sentence set a course for the therapy that follows. Often this
direction is not a useful one, and the therapist will later complain that
the client is resistant or "passive-aggressive," not realizing that this
behavior is a predictable response to the therapist's own presuppositions. By sensitizing ourselves to our own presuppositions, we can
find ways in which we may have been holding our clients back

unknowingly, and we can use this information to generate more helpful presuppostions.

It is impossible to avoid using presuppositions. Every sentence we utter sends many signals to our clients by what we presuppose. The more we know about how we send these messages, the more power and impact every word can have.

Training in presuppositions also sensitizes therapists to the presuppositions in what clients say, pointing out exactly where their thinking is limited, and often suggesting what can be done to make it easier for them to have the new perspectives and responses they want.

Presuppositions of Time

Every sentence has a verb tense, which carries a time message to the client, and these can be particularly powerful. The past cannot be changed. While we can change our *present memories* of the past and our *evaluations* of the past with great benefit, most people usually perceive the past as fixed and unchangeable. However, the future is ripe with possibilities and alternatives.

Perhaps a wife says, "We always fight. It's a terrible problem in our relationship. And if the fight gets intense, he always hits me."

This woman is speaking of the problem as occurring *throughout time.* "We *always fight.*" "He *always hits* me." "It *is* a problem." This lets us know that she is thinking of the problem existing in the past, present, and future. Even though she is using present tense, the "always" indicates that she is generalizing throughout time. In contrast, she could have said, "He hit me when we fought on Saturday," which would limit the problem to a narrow and contextualized *past* segment of time.

My response to the wife might be, "So this *has been* a terrible problem. Each time you *have gotten* in fights, your husband *has hit* you." With these words, I am letting the wife know I understand what she has said. More important, however, the verb tense describes the problem in a way that *leaves* it in the past. Next I can begin to direct her thinking toward what she wants in the future—"And I'm guessing you both want things to be different."

Notice the difference in your experience if you think of some minor difficulty of your own, and say this sentence to yourself: "It *is* a problem, *isn't* it?"

Now try saying, "That *has been* a problem, *hasn't* it?"

If you pay attention to your internal images as you do this, you will find that the location of your image of the problem shifts with each sentence. Typically the image of "It is a problem . . . " is more in front of you, closer, and associated, while your image of "That has been a problem . . . " is more to the side, farther away, and dissociated. Both sentences match your experience, but the second one leaves the problem *out of the future*, and literally clears the way for new behavior in a subtle, yet profound, way. If we use every sentence to communicate subtly that problems are unlikely to continue into the future, and that solutions are part of the future, we make it easier for our clients to develop and consider solutions.

Many therapies and therapists still direct their primary attention toward the past. While it is possible to speak of the past in a way that puts useful presuppositions in place, *it is much easier to slide in presuppositions of things being different, better, or solved in the future and present.* Even a brilliant therapist is operating with both hands tied behind his back if he limits himself to changing presuppositions about the past.

For example, let's say a client wants to lose weight. If I try to presuppose this problem has been solved in the past, I might say, "When did you first notice that you had solved your weight problem?" Since this presupposition is in direct contrast to the client's sense of what's real, it won't work. The client is likely to conclude that I'm crazy or stupid, rather than find it easier to change. "Anyone can see I'm still overweight!"

However, since the future hasn't happened yet, it is much more malleable. It's the easiest place to begin to put in presuppositions about change without violating the client's sense of reality. "What resources do you think *will allow you to lose weight easily?*"; "What *will be* your first indication that you *have* what you need to maintain your desired weight?"; "After you *reach* and *maintain* your desired weight, do you think you will *look back* and find it strange that you were ever overweight, or do you think you *will have* a feeling of understanding and compassion toward that old you?" Once the client begins to think of his desired outcome as something that almost inevitably will occur, it becomes easier to develop specific interventions to accomplish the desired outcome.

Here is a more detailed example of how to use time presuppositions to set the stage for change:

CLIENT: I *feel* like I can't stand up for myself with my husband. If I did, he'd think I was disrespectful. *Whenever* he *tells* me what he wants, I just *feel* overwhelmed, and I feel I *should* do it. But *I'm mad* about it at the same time.

Although this client doesn't say "always," she is speaking of the problem as continuing through time.

THERAPIST: So up *until this point in time*, you *haven't been* able to stand up for yourself the way you want to. You've often *felt* like you should do what he wants, but then you *have been* mad about it at the same time.

This restatement of the problem limits it to the past.

And how *will* you *be* responding differently when you *are responding* in a way that is fully satisfying to you?

Using "will be" asks the client to think of the solution in the future; "are responding" moves the solution into the present by shifting the verb tense. Later in the session, the therapist might put the problem even more completely into the past, and solidify the solution by saying, "Is it that you *hadn't* noticed the way in which your standing up for yourself is actually more respectful of your husband? Do you think that's what *kept* you from *automatically expressing your own desires* in the past?"

After some practice, you will find yourself combining different presuppositional forms and time frames into even more powerful messages. "How many times do you think you will have touched Billy lovingly when you first realize that it was this touching that makes him feel the strength of your love and connection with him?"

That sentence may seem a little unwieldy when you read it, because combined presuppositions have a hypnotic effect, particularly when they include several temporal shifts. The sentence starts in the present, goes into the future with "will," moves back into an earlier future with "have touched," goes back to the future with "when," heads into the more distant future with "first" (since it presupposes second and successive times), and moves back into the (future) past with "was," which is then transformed into the present with "makes." For a more in-depth discussion of this kind of use of verb tenses, see Chapter Two of *Change Your Mind—and Keep the Change* (1987).

Nonverbal Presuppositions

A variety of studies have probed the relative importance of verbal and nonverbal communication. Although these studies come up with different numbers, they all agree that the nonverbal component of communication is far more important than the verbal, imparting from 65 percent to 85 percent of the total impact. Although the nonverbal delivery of a presupposition is at least as important as its verbal construction, developing flexibility in nonverbal behavior is completely omitted from most therapy training.

For instance, in spoken English, questions end with a rising pitch, while statements do not. Commands typically end with a sinking pitch. If you ask, "How much do you love him?" and allow your voice to sink at the end, the apparent question covertly takes on the impact of a command, strengthening the presupposition that "you love him." Although most people respond strongly to such tonal communications, very few are able to recognize them consciously; this increases their impact.

Marking out part of a sentence that is presupposed or that constitutes a command with a gesture or by shifting voice tone or volume—or all of these—adds additional impact.

Although these "embedded commands" were an explicit part of Milton Erickson's work, few people use them systematically, particularly in the absence of a formal trance induction. Virginia Satir, however, is one of the few therapists who used them fully, and this contributed significantly to her effectiveness.

Trainees can easily be sensitized to the impact of their nonverbal behavior in experiential exercises during which they can experiment. Trios consisting of client, therapist, and observer provide opportunities to identify how specific nonverbal behaviors support or interfere with the delivery of presuppositions (or any other intervention).

In the therapist role, trainees try out alternative behaviors and observe their impact on the client. In the client role, they become sensitive to their subjective responses to specific communications. This develops sensitivity to what clients experience, and indicates which specific nonverbal behaviors to watch for in clients. In the observer role, trainees learn to watch the nonverbal interaction between client and therapist, and notice what they both miss.

In both client and observer roles, trainees can provide specific feedback to the therapist, particularly demonstrations of alternative ways to communicate nonverbally.

How Presuppositions Work

Although linguists have described presuppositions for many years, until recently no one has explored how they actually work to change subjective experience.

One of the most frequently used types of presupposition is called "subordinate clauses of time," using such words as before, after, during, as, since, when, prior, while, etc. These words can help create presupposed sequences or links between experiences in time (in contrast to explicit, conscious links). It's actually easy to discover how presuppositions work; all it takes is paying close attention to your own internal images. For example, here is an experiment from *Change Your Mind—and Keep the Change* (1987, pp. 31-32).

> Try the following experiment. First make a representation of "eating dinner at a restaurant." . . . Then make a representation of "discussing a proposal." . . . Now notice your internal experience of the following sentence: "Let's eat dinner at a restaurant before discussing a proposal." . . . Notice how the two representations become smoothly linked together in your mind. Unless you are adept at identifying presuppositions, this process occurs unconsciously. (Try reading that sentence *without* linking those two representations.) Now try a slightly different sentence: "Before we discuss a proposal, let's eat dinner at a restaurant." In this case, the first representation you make, "discussing a proposal," moves aside to

your less-detailed peripheral visual field, in order to make room for "eating dinner at a restaurant." In each case the result is the same; the presupposed representation becomes linked to the other, more conscious one. The process of getting there is slightly different, due to the different order of the two sentences.

Now try using the word "as." Notice how you represent the sentence, "As we discuss the proposal, let's eat dinner at a restaurant." Now try the reversed sentence: "Let's eat dinner at a restaurant as we discuss the proposal." With both of these sentences, the two representations blend together into the same time-frame. Most people find the first sentence easier to process, because the very first word, "as," notifies your mind that you will be putting two representations together. The second sentence requires you to go back and change the representation you started with after it's already formed.

If you go on to experiment with the other time words listed above, you can discover for yourself how they alter your representations to link them together in your mind.

Although we can learn to focus on these subtle subjective events, in normal conversation we respond to them without being consciously aware of them. This is the source of their power.

When you know how different kinds of presuppositions affect subjective experience, you can decide what subjective experience you want to induce in a client, and then choose the presuppositions that will have the desired impact.

Sensory Feedback

After you have crafted a presupposition and delivered it exquisitely, it's important to be able to observe whether it has had the desired effect. Ultimately, "The proof of the pudding is in the eating," and the effectiveness of a presupposition is measured not by how clever it is, but by the response it elicits in the client.

Again, nonverbal responses will usually tell you much more than the verbal. Sometimes nonverbal responses will be obvious, and sometimes they will be subtle. However, they will always be present, and detection is a function of two factors: 1) the therapist's sensory acuity—the ability to *discriminate* small shifts in posture, breathing, muscle tone, facial expression, etc., and 2) the therapist's ability to *elicit* robust responses through the therapist's own nonverbal expressive behavior.

When communicating with preverbal children, or with animals, you can use words, but since such children and animals don't know the meaning of the words, they are irrelevant. They will only respond to nonverbal tone, tempo, volume, etc. It is this nonverbal expressiveness that communicates the love, caring, and connection that the preverbal child experiences.

Experience with preverbal children or animals gives a therapist essential nonverbal skills for behavioral change. With that basis established, you can think of using language in the same way you have learned to use all your other behavior—*as a way to elicit appropriate responses* in the client. The next step is to link those responses, and contextualize them by linking them to appropriate cues. Virginia Satir's work demonstrates all these skills, and they can be taught in simple experiential exercises to add power to verbal presuppositions.

Appendix II
Physical Contact

In the videotape "Of Rocks and Flowers" (1983), Virginia works with a blended family in which the couple has been married for a year. Bob, a recovering alcoholic, is the father of the two children, four-year-old Aaron and two-year-old Robbie. The children's biological mother had abused them repeatedly—pushing them down stairs, tying them up under the sink, etc. The father describes taking the children to the hospital for treatment of bruises and cigarette burns thirteen times during the last year of his previous marriage. The mother is currently under psychiatric treatment and doesn't visit the children.

Aaron and Robbie are highly active children who have demonstrated violent behavior: slapping and spanking babies, and on two occasions holding a baby down and choking it.

Betty, 27, was abused by her previous husband, who was also an alcoholic. She is pregnant, and is acutely afraid that the boys will abuse her own child after it is born. If the children's violent behavior does not stop, she fears that she might have to leave the marriage to protect her child.

This is a revised version of an article, "Getting in Touch, with Virginia" that originally appeared in *Anchor Point: The International Journal for Effective NLP Communicators,* Vol. 3, No. 1, January 1989.

If you have a pretty grim picture of this family at this point, you are only partly right. Although the parents are stuck and unhappy, the children are spontaneous and expressive. They also express the anger and violence that they have been exposed to. The parents, acting out of frustration and fear, respond to them roughly, which tends to increase the children's violence.

Throughout the session, Virginia demonstrates how she wants the parents to touch and respond to the children. She puts her hand lightly on a shoulder or on one or both knees when she is talking to one of the children, sometimes also patting or squeezing. At one point she gently cradles Aaron's chin with her fingertips, waiting patiently to talk to him until she has his full attention. At other times she touches a child's wrist or holds his hand gently while talking to the parents. Soon she begins touching the parents in the same way.

Virginia always insisted on using touch to be sure the message is attended to—by both the sender and receiver. For example, at one point she asks Bob (verbatim), "Do you anticipate any difficulty in helping Aaron and Robbie to understand why they can't go to see their [biological] mother?"

When he expresses uncertainty, Virginia first suggests what to say: "There is a difference between saying . . . that here is a lady who hurts you and gets angry and doesn't know what she's doing. That's a different thing from saying that she's no good."

When he agrees, she goes on to suggest action.

"And let me see, at this moment, if you're willing to say to each of your sons that right now that they will not be able to see their mother because she hurts them, and you have to wait until she knows how to deal with herself better. Because, see, that's the same problem as what you're trying to get them (the children) to do—that they may not hurt, and you are protecting them from being hurt, and I wonder how you would feel just moving up to this son of yours and saying to him—"

When Bob starts to talk without moving, Virginia insists on adding touch. "No. Come up here. Come up here and just come up front to front with him (gesturing to Bob and pulling Aaron's chair toward Bob) and take his hands. And move it (the chair), can you move up a little bit more? Now take both his hands and tell him that."

After some work with the parents, Virginia spends some time alone with the two children:

VIRGINIA (to Aaron, her hands on his sides): Do you have good feelings about Betty?

AARON (distracted): No, uh, well, my Mom and Dad they make me— (He turns toward Robbie.) Robbie makes me mad.

VIRGINIA (taking his hand and pulling him toward her): Look at me, now. I am asking you about you and Betty.

AARON (bringing his left hand up to Virginia's cheek): My Mom and Dad they give me a nice (Virginia places her hand over Aaron's, and he brings his right hand up to the other side of her face.)—place for you. (It is interesting to note that the child actually initiates the face-touching; now Virginia uses it to bring the family back together.)

VIRGINIA: I like the way you touch my face. (Virginia gently holds both of Aaron's wrists.) Touch it really gently. That's right. Could you touch Betty's face gently like that? (Aaron touches his own face, nodding as he does.) OK. Gently? (*Aaron:* Ah huh.) All right. I am going to put this (a paper she has been holding) away. (She takes both his hands and places them on her face again.) Look at me now. And touch my face again gently. Does that feel good to you? (Aaron nods.) Let me touch your face gently like that. (She puts her hands on his face.) Does that feel good?

AARON: Ah huh. (He turns and begins to talk to Robbie.)

VIRGINIA (taking him by the shoulders and gently turning him back to face her): Look at, look at, look at me now. (Aaron's head moves forward in a pucker.) You don't have to worry (Virginia kisses him quickly on the lips) about him (Robbie) right now. (*Aaron:* OK.) But I would like for you—if you know how, and I have shown you how now—to put your hands on Betty's face gently (Virginia puts her hands on Aaron's cheeks again, and Aaron puts his hands on Virginia's cheeks) and to have her feel the good feeling of your hands and you can feel her hands. Could you do that?

AARON (cheerfully): OK.

VIRGINIA: Great, now sit down here for a minute now. (Robbie is turned away, playing with a cup on a low table. Virginia gently pulls on Robbie's shoulder.) Robbie, come here, honey. Take your finger out of the cup. I like that when you do that. (She takes his hands briefly.) Look at me now. (She puts both her hands on the sides of his chest.) Can you put your hands on my face? (Robbie looks up and puts his left hand on her cheek.) Both hands on my face like this. (She places his other hand on her other cheek and holds both his wrists.) Like that. Does that feel good?

ROBBIE (nodding): Yes. Yes.

VIRGINIA (as she puts her hands on his cheeks): All right, now let me, let me put my hands on your face. Look at me now. Does that feel good? Now I am going to ask your Mommy to come up here: Betty . . . (Betty and Bob return; Bob is off-camera.) Now would you take your beautiful little hands and put them on Betty's face like that. (She shows him with her own hands.) Would you do that? Just like that? (Robbie puts his hands on Betty's face briefly.) Do it some more like that. (She shows him again.) Just hold her like—beautiful, just hold her little face. (Virginia supports Robbie's arm, and Betty also puts her hands on Robbie's face.) Now, could you give her at this moment—(Robbie laughs) let her feel you, too?

AARON (reaching toward Betty's face): Now let me feel you.

VIRGINIA (to Aaron): Now wait, wait one minute. (Virginia gently pushes down on Aaron's arm, and turns back to Robbie. Betty's hands are still on Robbie's face.) Now do you think that you could—many times a day—come up to this lovely lady and give her your hands like that? Could you do that? (Virginia shows him again with one hand, and Robbie copies her.) Could you do that? Now would you come over here, Robbie, (Virginia draws Robbie to one side with both hands, and then encircles him with her left arm) and Aaron, will you sit over here? (*Aaron*: Yes.) Right here. (Virginia gestures to the chair and guides him with her hand on his shoulder as he sits down.)

ROBBIE: Can I sit by—

VIRGINIA (to Robbie): And you just stand where you are. (to Aaron) Now could you lean over (Virginia shows him with her hands) and put your lovely soft hands on your mother's face, and feel it, just feel it.

AARON (smiling, to Betty): Is that pretty?

BETTY (softly): Um hmn.

AARON: Now feel mine. (Betty puts her hands on Aaron's face.)

ROBBIE: I can run far!

VIRGINIA: Yeah, I know. (to Aaron) OK, now. You liked that. And I saw Betty liked that, too.

AARON: Now shake hands now, Mom. (Aaron extends his hand and Betty shakes hands with him. Aaron turns to Virginia.) You shake hands too. (Virginia shakes his left hand with her left.)

VIRGINIA (to Aaron, still holding his left hand):   Yes, OK. Now what I would like to find out from you is, could you remember (stroking his forehead, brushing his hair aside with her right hand) that you could, you could put your hands so beautifully on your mother's face. (Virginia puts her right hand on Betty's face.)

AARON: Uh hum. (Aaron puts his right hand on his mother's face in the same way that Virginia did.)

VIRGINIA: Both hands like this (demonstrating) so you hold her. (Aaron uses both hands.) Hold her face.

AARON: I hold you. (He smiles and kisses Betty, and then hugs her, as Robbie kisses Virginia, and they hug.)

VIRGINIA: Now I would like to have your Daddy come in. (Bob sits down and starts to put on his microphone.) Now your daddy has a lot of hair on his face, if you'll notice. (Virginia has one hand on Robbie's back and one gently holding Aaron's wrist.) What you'd like to just make those pretty hands to go around his face like that (demonstrating) so you can feel the touch.

AARON (putting his hands on Bob's face):   Is that pretty, Daddy?

BOB (still distracted by putting on his microphone):   Uh huh. (Aaron kisses Bob.)

VIRGINIA (keeping one hand around Robbie's waist):   Now could you ask your Daddy if he would do that with you?

AARON: Would you do that with me? (Bob says "sure" and puts his hands on Aaron's face, and then kisses him. Aaron laughs excitedly.) Do that with me! (Robbie approaches Betty and touches her face, and she reaches out in response.)

VIRGINIA (reaching for Aaron's hand):   Now this may sound very strange. (Robbie moves forward to Bob and reaches out toward his face.) Yes, it is time for you too, to feel—put your hands on your Daddy's face (demonstrating). Both of them, like you were holding something very special. Because that's there too. (Robbie crawls into

Bob's lap, and Aaron crawls into Betty's lap, as Virginia talks to the parents.)

Those little hands know a lot of things; they need to be re-educated. OK. Now, there is a lot of energy in both these youngsters, like there is in both of you. And I am going to talk to your therapist about making some room for you to have some respite (from the children). But use every opportunity you can to get this kind of physical contact. And what I would also recommend that you do is that the two of you are clear about what you expect.

And if you (Bob) could learn from Betty how to pay attention (to the kids) more quickly. I would like you to be able to get over your message without a "don't" in it, without a "don't"—and that your strength of your arms when you pick them up—I don't know if I can illustrate it to you, but let me have your arm for a minute (reaching for Bob's forearm). Let me show you the difference. Pick up my arm like you were going to grab me. (Bob grabs her arm.) All right. Now when you do that, my muscles all start to tighten, and I want to hit back. (Bob nods.) Now pick up my arm like you wanted to protect me. (Bob holds her arm.) All right. I feel your strength now, but I don't feel like I want to pull back like this. (*Bob*: Yeah.)

And what I'd like you to do is to do *lots* and lots of touching of both of these children. And when things start (to get out of hand), then you go over—don't say anything—go over to them and just take them, (demonstrating the protective holding on both Robbie's forearms) but you have to know in your inside that you're not pulling them (Aaron briefly puts his hands on top of Virginia's and Robbie's arms) like this (demonstrating), but you are taking them in a strong way, (stroking Bob's arm with both hands) like you saw the difference. I'll demonstrate it to you, (Bob) too. First of all I am going to grab you (demonstrating) like that. (*Bob*: Yeah.) You see you want to pull back. All right. Now, at this time what I am going to do is give you some strength. (demonstrating holding his arm with both hands. Robbie pats Virginia's hand) But I am not going to ask you to retaliate. Now this is the most important thing for you to start with.

(Virginia turns to Betty and offers her forearm.) OK. Now I'd like to do the same with you. So, take my arm really tight, just— (Betty grabs Virginia's arm, and Aaron does, too.) Yeah, that's right, like you really wanted to give me "what for." OK. All right. Now give it to me like you want to give me support, but you also want to give me a boundary. (Aaron reaches toward Betty's hand and Virginia takes Aaron's hand in her free hand.) It's a little bit tight, a little bit tight.

(Robbie holds Virginia's other arm with both hands, copying Betty's way of holding.) Now (Betty) try doing it from the bottom and putting your other hand on the top. (Betty holds with both hands.) All right. Now, you're squeezing me a little bit too much, but I won't react. I don't feel like I want to do that (pulling back). These are how bodies react. (Aaron plays with Virginia's watch.)

So the next time you see anything coming, what you do is you go and make that contact, (Virginia demonstrates by holding Aaron's upper arm) and then let it go soft. (Virginia takes Aaron's hands and begins to draw him out of Betty's lap.) Now, Aaron, I'd like you to come up here so I could demonstrate something to your mother for a minute. (*Aaron*: OK.) Just move over here to the side; you won't have to go too long. Now, let's suppose some moment I'm not thinking and I take you like that (grabbing Betty's arms suddenly with both hands). You see what you want to do? (Betty nods.) All right. Now I am going to do it another way. I am giving you the same message, (Virginia holds Betty's arm firmly with both hands, looking directly into her eyes, and starts to stand up) but I am doing it like this. And I am looking at you, and I'm giving you a straight message. OK. Now your body at that point is not going to respond negatively to me. It is going to feel stopped, but not negative. And then I will take you like this. (Virginia puts one arm around Betty's back and the other under her upper arm.) Just get up now. (Betty stands up.) I take you like this. I've got you like this (Virginia puts both arms around Betty and draws her close) and now I will hold you. I will hold you like that for a little bit.

Following the session, in an interview with Ramon Corrales of the Family Therapy Institute of Kansas City, Virginia comments explicitly on her touching, both in this session and generally. (See pages 38-39 for this commentary.)

Appendix III
Eye Accessing Cues

While most people lump their internal information processing together and call it "thinking," Richard Bandler and John Grinder have noted that it can be useful to divide thinking into the different *sensory modalities* in which it occurs.

When we process information internally, we can do it visually (sight), auditorily (hearing), kinesthetically (feeling), olfactorily (smell), or gustatorily (taste). As you read the word "circus," you may know what it means by seeing images of circus rings, elephants, or trapeze artists; by hearing carnival music; by feeling the hard seats, or the child on your lap, or by feeling excited; or by smelling and tasting popcorn or cotton candy. The meaning of a word can be perceived in any one, or in any combination, of these five sensory channels.

Bandler and Grinder have also observed that people move their eyes in systematic directions, depending upon the kind of thinking they are doing. These movements are called *eye accessing cues*, and they are evident in both Virginia Satir and Linda as they interact in the videotape from which the transcript in this book was taken. These accessing cues provide additional valuable information about how a person is experiencing events internally.

The chart (next page) indicates the kind of processing most people are doing when they are moving their eyes in a particular direction. About 5 percent of individuals are "reversed," that is, they move their eyes in a mirror image of this chart.

The chart is easiest to use if you superimpose it over someone's face, so that as you see a person looking in a particular direction you can visualize the label for that eye accessing cue.

As you watch the videotape of Virginia's work with Linda, you can see clear indications of Virginia's internal accessing. She often looked up and to her left to see an internal image—either an image of what Linda has just said, or a picture of what Virginia will do next. Virginia also frequently looked down and to her left when recalling what Linda had said earlier, or when thinking auditorily about what to say next. Since Virginia accessed feelings very quickly—directly from her internal pictures and words—you seldom observe her looking down and to her right.

Linda also looked up and to her left a lot for remembered images, and less often down and to her left for recalling words. Linda also looked up and to her right when visualizing images she hasn't actually seen—when thinking of how she would like to be different in the future, for instance, or thinking over a new way of seeing her mother. Many of these eye movements are noted in the transcript, particularly near the beginning.

Although these cues are not essential to understanding Virginia's session with Linda, they do provide an additional perspective, allowing you to track internal processes that are not otherwise observable.

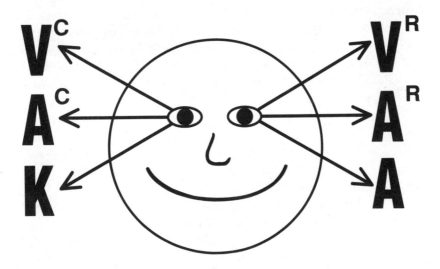

V^r **Visual remembered**: seeing images of things seen before, in the way they were seen before. Questions that usually elicit this kind of accessing include: "What color are your mother's eyes?" "What does your coat look like?"

V^c **Visual constructed**: seeing images of things never seen before, or seeing things differently from how they were seen before. An example of a question that usually elicits this kind of processing is: "What would an orange hippopotamus with purple spots look like?"

A^r **Auditory remembered**: remembering sounds heard before. A question that usually elicits this kind of processing is: "What is the sound of your alarm clock?"

A^c **Auditory constructed**: hearing sounds not heard before. Questions that can elicit this kind of processing include: "What would the sound of clapping turning into the sound of birds singing sound like?" "What would your voice sound like an octave lower?"

A_d **Auditory digital**: talking to oneself. Questions that tend to elicit this kind of processing include: "Can you say something to yourself that you often say to yourself?" "Can you recite the Pledge of Allegiance to yourself?"

K **Kinesthetic**: feeling emotions, tactile sensations (sense of touch), or proprioceptive feelings (feelings of muscle movement). Questions to elicit this kind of processing include: "What does it feel like to be happy?" "What is the feeling of touching a pine cone?" "What does it feel like to run?"

Eye accessing cues are presented in more detail in *Frogs into Princes* (1979, pp. 19-27).

Appendix IV
A Virginia Satir Meditation

During workshops, particularly at the end of the day, Virginia often offered what she called "meditations" or "processes." She asked people to find a comfortable position, close their eyes and relax. Often she played soothing music as she began to speak in a slow, clear voice.

Although Virginia often had harsh words for hypnosis because she disliked manipulation, these meditations contained the same kinds of verbal and nonverbal patterns and presuppositions as overt hypnotic inductions.

The meditation below is from *The Meditations of Virginia Satir*, by Anne and John Banmen (1991). First the entire meditation will be presented. Then it will be repeated with commentary, pointing out the verbal hypnotic patterns within the meditation that Virginia used to create empowering presuppositions about resources, capacities and choice.

Making Choices That Fit

As we look at our resources, be aware and appreciative of all the things we have seen and heard, felt, touched and smelled, all the thoughts and feelings that have been a part of our life up to this time, all of the choices and the words and the movements.

We have a great resource from which to choose.

And because we have chosen one way in the past does not mean we have to continue that way, but it could be one of the choices when we add other possibilities.

As we come fully in touch with our capacity, inborn in all of us, to choose, out of all we have at this moment, that which fits us well, we notice that there are things we haven't used.

Once they were very fitting, but now we can clear them out, sending them on their way with a blessing for what they did at that time.

No longer useful are thoughts such as, "I must never share my feelings or you will be hurt."

Maybe at one moment in time that did fit, but maybe it will never fit again.

If you were to find many things that you learned and no longer have any use for, could you allow yourself to choose to let them go with your blessing?

Once they served you well, but now they are no longer necessary.

And could you look at what you have that fits you well?

Honor it and give yourself permission to add to yourself that which you need or want which you still do not have.

As you allow yourself to look again at your resources, become more fully aware that they are there for your constant use.

That you are the one who not only selects what you will use, but you will select how you use them.

And could you, while you are doing this, also give yourself permission to let go of everything except the experience you can use for learning that will make your present illuminated.

Making Choices That Fit: Commentary

As we look at our resources, be aware and appreciative of all the things we have seen and heard, felt, touched and smelled, all the thoughts and feelings that have been a part of our life up to this time, all of the choices and the words and the movements.

"As" presupposes that listeners have unspecified resources and are looking at them. "As" also presupposes the rest of the sentence. "Be aware and appreciative" is a direct command that also presupposes what follows. This is an example of nested presuppositions. "Be aware and appreciative" is nested within "as."

Everything Virginia says is at a very general and universal level, making it adaptable to each person's specific world. Everyone has "things we have seen and heard, felt, touched and smelled," etc. However, most people are not appreciative of all that has happened in their lives. Being appreciative is an important first step toward greater self-acceptance and willingness to examine and change what hasn't worked.

Including choices among past events is also important. Many people do not experience much choice in their lives. They think their decisions are forced on them by others or events, and this contributes to feelings of powerlessness and victimization. Thinking of past events as choices empowers people by putting them into the active role of choosing.

This theme of actively choosing is presupposed or restated throughout this meditation. By immediately following "choices" with "and the words and the movements"—things we have all experienced—Virginia maximizes the likelihood that the listener will also accept "choices."

We have a great resource from which to choose.

Choosing is presupposed in the present. Even if the listener discounts having a *great* resource, having a resource is still presupposed.

And because we have chosen one way in the past does not mean we have to continue that way, but it could be one of the choices when we add other possibilities.

Choosing is presupposed in the past. By saying that choosing in the past does not mean we have to continue that way, Virginia contradicts a presupposition many people have: that the past habitually continues to determine the present. Since many people might reject this statement, Virginia follows this with a "but" that negates it, then offers a new statement that an old choice could continue to be a choice "when we add other possibilities." Adding other possibilities is presupposed and linked to the possibility of using the old choice.

Overall, this sentence leaves the listener with two choices: 1) Choosing not to use old choices when we no longer want to, and 2) Continuing to use the old choice and adding other possibilities. Both these choices are empowering by presupposing the ability to choose and change.

As we come fully in touch with our capacity, inborn in all of us, to choose out of all we have at this moment, that which fits us well, we notice that there are things we haven't used.

This sentence is a beautiful example of multiple presuppositions at multiple levels—in this case seven, with each level nested within others. To simplify analysis, let's take the first part of the sentence up to the word "well."

1. "As" presupposes the rest of the sentence.

2. "We come fully" presupposes that we are already in touch with what follows.

3. "In touch with" presupposes our inborn capacity to choose.

4. "To choose" presupposes all that follows.

5. "That which" presupposes that some alternatives will "fit us well."

6. "All" presupposes multiple alternative choices or resources that "we have at this moment."

If we were to summarize the levels of presupposition in this sentence from the inside out we could say:

7. We have many choices now.

6. Some of these choices/resources fit us.

5. Some of these will fit us well.

4. We can choose among them.

3. We are already in touch with this ability to choose.

2. We are becoming fully in touch with this ability.

1. All this is happening now.

Nested presuppositions are difficult to recognize, even when studying them in written form. They are even more difficult to notice when listening to them. Yet we have no difficulty understanding the meaning of what is said, because our processing of language is so automatic and unconscious.

By using the word "fits," Virginia deftly bypasses judgments about good and bad, as well as all the anguish and confusion that follow such judgments. In the last part of the sentence, Virginia presupposes that the listener will notice "there are things we haven't used," which has a double meaning. This statement can mean noticing useful choices and resources that haven't been utilized, or it can mean noticing old behaviors that are no longer used. Both meanings are empowering. The first one sends us on a search for useful choices and possibilities available to us that we haven't used; the second provides counterexamples to the idea that habitual behaviors are hard to change.

Once they were very fitting, but now we can clear them out, sending them on their way with a blessing for what they did at that time.

Virginia says that old choices were fitting in the past, and follows with a "but" that negates this "now"—implying that they no longer fit. Since they no longer fit, we can actively choose to "send them on their way." By adding "with a blessing for what they did at that time," Virginia returns to the idea that old behaviors were fitting choices at the time they were developed. This establishes a new meaning for problem behaviors. They aren't perverse demonstrations of our stupidity; they are simply out-of-date examples of our positive ability to cope and learn. The impact of this reframe is twofold:

1. The Behavioral Level. Rather than rejecting and fighting a problem behavior, we can accept it, appreciate it, learn from it, and add the new possibilities that Virginia referred to earlier.

2. The Self-Esteem Level. Rather than feeling depressed, or berating ourselves for problem behaviors, we can feel good about ourselves and our abilities to learn and cope.

No longer useful are thoughts such as, "I must never share my feelings or you will be hurt."

Now Virginia turns from the general to the more specific: hiding feelings is no longer useful, though it may have been at one time.

Maybe at one moment in time that did fit, but maybe it will never fit again.

Since "maybe" refers only to possibility, the listener can easily make a representation of what Virginia says without having to agree or disagree. By using "maybe" to refer first to the past and then to the future, Virginia links the two time frames. If the listener agrees to the first "maybe" this will tend to transfer agreement to the second "maybe" that refers to the behavior not fitting in the future.

If you were to find many things that you learned and no longer have any use for, could you allow yourself to choose to let them go with your blessing?

Using "if" creates a gentle "as–if" frame; it's also the first part of an "if-then" causal linkage. "Allow yourself" is an embedded command that presupposes that the rest of the sentence will occur if only the listener allows it, and this is embedded within a conversational postulate: "Could you allow yourself...?" "Choose to let them go with your blessing" is also an embedded command.

Once they served you well, but now they are no longer necessary.

Virginia reiterates that old behaviors were useful in the past, negates this in the present with "but now," and describes them as "no longer necessary," a nonjudgmental term that implies we can simply and easily let go of them.

And could you look at what you have that fits you well?

Using a conversational postulate to introduce an embedded command, Virginia suggests looking at our presupposed successes: the behaviors that do fit and satisfy us.

Honor it and give yourself permission to add to yourself that which you need or want which you still do not have.

"Honor it" is a direct command to respect our behaviors that do work, and by implication also to honor ourselves for our capacities. "Give yourself permission" is a direct command that presupposes that what follows will occur if we don't interfere: "Add to yourself that which you need or want which you still do not have" is also an embedded command.

"Still" is an important word here. First, it presupposes that the listener has already successfully added many experiences that were needed or wanted in the past. "Still" also implies that it will happen in the future. "Still" is very similar in meaning to "yet," which more strongly implies that the future will be different. "That which you need or want which you do not have yet" would be an even stronger statement presupposing future change.

As you allow yourself to look again at your resources, become more fully aware that they are there for your constant use.

The first part of the sentence contains three levels of nested presuppositions. "As" presupposes all of what follows. "Allow yourself" presupposes that what follows will occur without effort if you permit it. "Again" presupposes that you have looked at resources before, making it easy to do it again. "Become more fully aware that they are there for your constant use" is a direct command that also contains three levels of nested presupposition: 1) "More" presupposes "fully." 2) "Fully" presupposes "aware." 3) "Aware" presupposes the rest of the sentence: "that they (presupposed resources) are there for your constant use." The implication is that all we have to do is choose to use our resources.

That you are the one who not only selects what you will use, but you will select how you use them.

"That you are" connects this sentence to the previous one and includes it within the previous set of nested presuppositions: "as you allow yourself" and "become more fully aware." Embedded in these nested presuppositions is the statement, "You are the one who not only selects what you will do." "Not only" presupposes that the listener will also do something else, followed with a "but" that clears the mind for the direct command that follows: "You will select how you use them."

And could you, while you are doing this, also give yourself permission to let go of everything except the experience you can use for learning that will make your present illuminated.

"While" presupposes the entire sentence, which is in the form of a conversational postulate. "Give yourself permission" is a direct command that presupposes that the following events will happen if only you agree to them: "Let go of everything except the experience you can use for learning that will make your present *illuminated*." The command "make your present *illuminated*" is embedded within the longer sentence, which is also a direct command. "Let go" presupposes that these unuseful experiences are now being held onto and that they will leave without effort when the effort of holding ceases.

Selected Bibliography

Andreas, Connirae and Andreas, Steve. *Heart of the Mind*. Moab, UT: Real People Press, 1989.

Andreas, Steve and Andreas, Connirae. *Change Your Mind—and Keep the Change*. Moab, UT: Real People Press, 1987.

Bandler, Richard. *Using Your Brain—for a CHANGE*. Moab, UT: Real People Press, 1985.

Bandler, Richard and Grinder, John. *Frogs into Princes*. Moab, UT: Real People Press, 1979.

——.*Reframing: Neuro-Linguistic Programming and the Transformation of Meaning*. Moab, UT: Real People Press, 1982.

——. *Patterns of the Hypnotic Techniques of Milton H. Erickson, M.D. vol. 1*. Cupertino, CA: Meta Publications, 1975.

——. *TRANCE-formations: Neuro-Linguistic Programming and the Structure of Hypnosis*. Moab, UT: Real People Press, 1981.

——. *The Structure of Magic, Vols. I and II*. Palo Alto, CA: Science and Behavior Books, 1975.

——, and Satir, Virginia. *Changing with Families*. Palo Alto, CA: Science and Behavior Books, 1976.

Banmen, Anne and Banmen, John. *Meditations of Virginia Satir.* Palo Alto, CA: Science and Behavior Books, forthcoming 1991.

Satir, Virginia. *Conjoint Family Therapy.* Palo Alto, CA: Science and Behavior Books, 1983.

——. *The New Peoplemaking.* Palo Alto, CA: Science and Behavior Books, 1988.

——. "Family Relations," a series of seven videotapes. NLP Comprehensive, 2897 Valmont Rd., Boulder, CO 80301. 1989.

——. "Of Rocks and Flowers," a videotape. Golden Triad Films, Inc. 100 Westport Sq. 4200 Pennsylvania, Kansas City, MO 64111. 1983.

——. "On Intimate Relationships," a set of 18 audiotapes. Creative Audio, 8751 Osborne, Highland, IN 46322. 1984.

——. and Baldwin, Michele. *Satir Step by Step: A Guide to Creating Change in Families.* Palo Alto, CA: Science and Behavior Books, 1983.

Index

About the Author

Steve Andreas, and his wife Connirae, are internationally known trainers and researchers in Neuro-Linguistic Programming (NLP). They are the co-directors of NLP Comprehensive, through which they conduct training seminars and Certification Programs, and also produce videotapes and audiotapes.

The Andreases have written two other books about NLP: *Heart of the Mind: Engaging Your Inner Power to Change With NLP* (1989) and *Change Your Mind—and Keep the Change* (1987). They have also edited four books by Richard Bandler and John Grinder, the co-developers of NLP: *Frogs into Princes* (1979), *TRANCE-formations* (1981), *Reframing* (1981), and *Using Your Brain—for a CHANGE* (1985).

Steve Andreas—under his former name, John O. Stevens—also wrote *Awareness: exploring, experimenting, experiencing*, based on his work with Fritz Perls and Gestalt Therapy. He also edited Fritz Perls' *Gestalt Therapy Verbatim*, Perls' autobiography *In and Out the Garbage Pail*, and Carl Rogers' book *Person to Person*, coauthored by his mother, Barry Stevens.

During the last six years the Andreases have focused principally on developing new patterns of intervention for personal change, and teaching them to others. They have developed specific processes for dealing with experiences of grief, shame, guilt, anger, resentment, and being criticized.

The Andreases live with their three young sons in Boulder, Colorado.